Robert W. Wingard

PAUL and the CORINTHIANS

The Life and Letters of Paul

Abingdon Press
Nashville

PAUL AND THE CORINTHIANS

Scripture quotations in this publication, unless otherwise indicated, are from the New Revised Standard Version of the Bible, copyrighted © 1989 by the Division of Christian Education of the National Council of the Churches of Christ in the United States of America, and are used by permission.

This book is printed on acid-free paper.

ISBN 0-687-07840-7

Art and Photo Credits: "Paul," by Diego Velázquez; "Corinth, Forum, and Lechaion Road" © 1986 Biblical Archaeology Society

02 03 04 05 06 07 08—10 9 8 7 6 5

MANUFACTURED IN THE UNITED STATES OF AMERICA

CONTENTS

INTRODUCTION: THE CHURCH AND THE BIBLE

I know a woman who has a severe case of Alzheimer's Disease. She remembers almost nothing about her past, sometimes not even recognizing her own son. Yet her physical body is in reasonably good condition for a person of her advanced years. Her son said to me, "This is not my mother. She looks and walks and sounds like my mother, but the person who gave birth to me and raised me with love no longer lives in this body. What is left is merely an empty shell."

When I remember what my friend said about his mother, I think about what is ailing mainline Protestant churches today. The United Methodists, the Presbyterians, the Episcopalians, and others are losing many thousands of members each year. No one is persecuting the church or trying to do it in. For the most part, American society today is indifferent toward the church. Many congregations have settled comfortably into a pattern that includes lots of wholesome activities but not much emphasis on spiritual depth. The young people enjoy recreational activities; the church bus gets used by the seniors to take trips to interesting places; the children are provided with excellent day care programs; and the stewardship committee manages to raise enough money to pay for it all. So what's the problem?

The problem is a little like Alzheimer's Disease. Our connection with our past has been broken, and we have lost the sense of our true identity as the church of Jesus Christ. Who are we, and what is our mission? What exactly is it that merited something as drastic as the crucifixion of God's own Son? And what is the relationship of our church here on Main Street USA to that earth-shattering event of long ago?

The Christian church in America recognizes and bewails its weakened state. There is no lack of diagnoses and prescriptions for what ails it. Books and articles come off the presses in a steady stream. Programs are being offered that promise to turn the church around and get it growing again. Such programs call for better marketing techniques, broader participation for all groups, more effective use of the media, or more intentional strategies for recruitment and retention of members. These programs are good, and no doubt they will help the churches gain some members. But do these programs address the real problem? Whether the church is thriving and growing among other institutions in society is not precisely the right question. It is more crucial to ask whether the church is finding effective ways to be what it is called to be and to do what it is called to do in the present generation. The American church must learn to function effectively in a cosmopolitan culture characterized by pluralism and secularism, and it must learn to do so without losing its distinctive identity and its God-given purpose.

The foundational thesis of this book is that the problems of the church in America today stem from a basic identity crisis and that solutions lie in the direction of a recovery of self and a rediscovery of mission, purpose, and character.

The church today needs to restore its continuity with the church of the New Testament and to do so in ways that will be compatible with current knowledge and experience.

Obviously this calls for Bible study. Members and leaders all across the church are recognizing this fact. Denominational publishers are providing new resources in print, audio, and video. Sunday school classes are seeking Bible-centered lessons, and Bible study groups of all ages are flourishing. Some of these efforts are very helpful, others are futile and fruitless, and still others tend to make matters worse by offering antiquated solutions to distinctly modern problems.

What is needed is not a "return" to the Bible but an "advance" to the Bible! God is always ahead of us, not behind us. The kingdom of God is found in the yet-to-be rather than in "the good ole days." The attempt to reconnect with the New Testament church must not be allowed to deteriorate into either sentimental nostalgia or inflexible biblicism.

What kind of Bible study do we need? What do we seek to gain from the New Testament? First of all, we need to rediscover Jesus himself—his life, his mission and message, the meaning of his death and resurrection, and the unique relationship to God that made him the Savior. Any renewal of the church in our time must first and foremost be Christ centered. Much work is being done today by scholars to uncover knowledge of the historical Jesus and to sharpen our picture of what actually happened in Palestine in the first century. Through sermons, lessons, studies, spiritual growth groups, and personal reading of Scripture, the church is seeking to bring Jesus Christ back into focused consciousness. This is the right way to go.

Second, we need to reestablish the connection between

the New Testament church and the church today. This present study is an attempt to do this by studying letters the apostle Paul wrote to his congregation in the city of Corinth in Greece. Paul is the premier leader of the New Testament church, and Corinth is a congregation among Paul's mission churches that offers close parallels to issues and concerns in today's congregations. For example, here are some of the characteristics of Corinthian society (Note the similarities to the contemporary world!):

- religious pluralism and rival cults
- a great variety of personal lifestyles
- confusion about standards of sexual activity
- a serious breakdown in family relationships
- drug abuse, especially the abuse of alcohol
- fascination with bizarre forms of behavior
- a widening gap between the rich and the poor
- a push toward the liberation of women from traditional roles

We should avoid oversimplification in our observance of rough parallels as we look at situations then and now in the church. We cannot merely adopt Paul's solution to a specific problem and apply it to the modern church. The fact that Paul said that "women should not speak in church" should not be used to deny clergy status to women. The fact that he said, "I will eat no meat" should not be used to demand that all true Christians be vegetarians. The fact that he said that "a woman should wear a veil on her head when she prays or prophesies" should not be used to set mandatory dress codes for modern worshipers. All these statements were made in response to very specific circumstances in Corinth, circumstances that cannot be duplicated

in a modern congregation or even in one of Paul's congregations. The church today can find more help from Paul in
its decision making by observing his method and his manner than by mimicking his specific conclusions.

This study seeks to do exactly that: to learn from Paul
by watching him in action and to gain insights about our
own issues and answers by observing the life of the
Corinthian congregation as revealed in Paul's letters
known to us as First and Second Corinthians. By sharing
with us his letters, Paul offers us the benefit of his own
experience, the experience of a fellow traveler in the Way.

I
CORINTH AND THE CORINTHIAN CHURCH

Paul's Arrival in Corinth

On his second missionary journey Paul pushed across the Aegean Sea to enter northern Greece. In keeping with his calling to be "the apostle to the Gentiles," Paul was responding to a request from a Macedonian (Macedonia was the region of northern Greece.) to "come over to Macedonia and help us" (Acts 16:9). As Paul entered Macedonia and traversed most of Greece from north to south organizing Christian groups and leaving them in the hands of local leaders, he was challenged by new and different cultures. Nowhere was this challenge more dramatic than in the large metropolis of Corinth.

Corinth was the capital of Achaia, the southern half of Greece. It was a city of almost half a million people located on the narrow isthmus that connects the main body of Greece with the Peloponnesus, the southern tip of the nation (see map on page 12). Corinth's location made it strategic to the east-west shipping lanes of the Mediterranean. The city had a port to the east (Cenchreae) and a port to the west (Lechaeon) connected at the narrowest point on the isthmus by only three miles of land. Small boats could be pulled across from one side to the other on wheels or runners, saving the long and hazardous 200-mile journey around the Peloponnesus. Larger vessels could

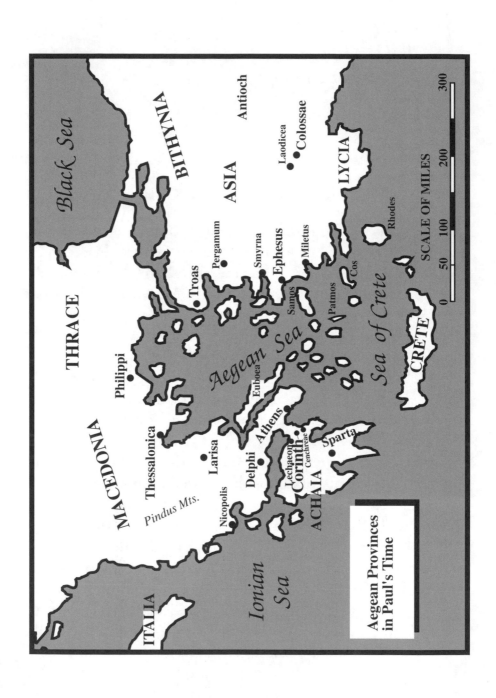

Aegean Provinces
in Paul's Time

SCALE OF MILES

0   50   100   200   300

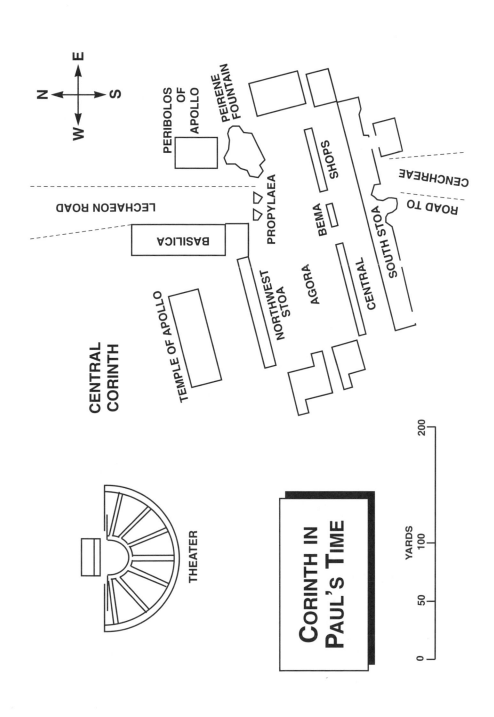

CENTRAL
CORINTH

TEMPLE OF APOLLO

THEATER

BASILICA

NORTHWEST STOA

AGORA

PROPYLAEA

LECHAEON ROAD

PERIBOLOS OF APOLLO

PEIRENE FOUNTAIN

BEMA

SHOPS

CENTRAL

SOUTH STOA

ROAD TO CENCHREAE

N
W — E
S

CORINTH IN
PAUL'S TIME

0   50   100   200

YARDS

unload their cargo at one port and reload it on a sister ship at the other port, swapping loads like modern airliners at a busy hub.

Corinth was a terminal city and consequently had an international and intercultural population. It was a major center for trade, banking, travel, and tourism. There were warehouses, inns, taverns, foreign food restaurants, souvenir shops, amusement parlors, and temples for the worship of every god imaginable.

This is the city Paul entered in A.D. 50 with the intention of offering Christ to one and all.

Paul found the Corinthians quite different from Athenians and other Greeks. At least part of the reason was the fact that the Greek city of Corinth had been destroyed and its citizens disbanded in 146 B.C. Mummius, a Roman general, had taken his army there to quell a rebellion against the Roman Empire. Mummius executed the men, made slaves of the women and children (to be utilized in other parts of the Empire), and burned and toppled all the buildings. One hundred years later, the Emperor Julius Caesar decided to use the beautiful, strategic site to construct a Roman city. He populated the city with former slaves ("freedmen"), homeless Greeks, sailors ready to retire from the sea, and various other persons from many different nations. Corinth quickly became the Roman commercial center and cosmopolitan culture that Paul encountered when he began what turned out to be an eighteen-month stay there (Acts 18:11).

Paul found many things in Corinth that were typically Roman. There were gymnasiums and athletic fields, testimony not only to the Roman love for spectator sports but also to the Greek love for participation in track and field games. The Isthmian Games, an early parallel to the Olympic Games, had been held in Greek Corinth before its destruction and were being revived by the citizenry of Roman Corinth. There were both indoor and outdoor theaters for the staging of dramas and other spectacles. There was a very large open market with several blocks of shops and booths, a kind of early "shopping center" along a paved road leading from the main city to the seaport.

The extent and variety of religious practices in Corinth must have fascinated Paul. There was "a church on every corner," so to speak. Temples had been built, priests ordained, and worshipers secured for many different cults. The members of the original Greek settlement seem to have worshiped Apollo. Seven of the thirty-eight pillars of the Temple of Apollo built by the Greeks in 550 B.C. are still standing today in the vicinity of the old marketplace (see map on page 13).

Towering 1500 feet above the city on the south is a steep mountain called Acrocorinth ("High Corinth"). This mountaintop with its magnificent 360-degree view was once considered sacred to Helios, the sun god. It is said that Helios was struck by the legendary beauty of Aphrodite, the goddess of love, and gave the mountaintop to her. (Her Roman name is Venus, made famous by the statue of Venus de Milo and other classical works of art.)

Aphrodite seems to have encouraged her followers to abandon warlike practices in favor of domestic bliss — an ancient version of the motto of the 1960's, "Make love, not war!" A temple for the worship of Aphrodite was built on top of Acrocorinth, and at the time of Paul there were several hundred "courtesans" who engaged worshipers in sexual pursuits as acts of homage to Aphrodite. No doubt, some of these women were little more than prostitutes using Aphrodite as a pretext to ply their trade; but there is evidence that others took seriously their function as priestesses of a goddess who proclaimed sexual satisfaction as a means toward peace on earth. The statue of Aphrodite in the temple at Acrocorinth depicted her conquering Ares, the god of war; it showed her using his shield as a mirror to fix her hair while she rested her bare foot coquettishly on his helmet. Ares was putting aside his sword. Some accounts say there was an inscription that read, "Love conquers War."

In 1993 and again in 1996, I climbed to the top of Acrocorinth to see for myself what remained of the Temple of Aphrodite. Information about the temple, its courtesans, and their activities is sparse and often conflicting; and systematic excavations have not been done. The ruins of the foundation of the temple indicate that it was very small, perhaps twenty-five feet wide and thirty-five feet long; but it must have appeared much larger because of the porches, columns, and steps on at least the three sides visible from ships on the seas. What an impression the white marble structure must have made on seafarers many miles away!

Imprinted coins and other items suggest that the temple contained a large statue of Aphrodite and perhaps one of Ares, the god of war, as well. Obviously there was no room for several hundred temple courtesans and their clients on the pinnacle or on the steep slopes surrounding it. Three hundred yards below the pinnacle there is a flattened area with thousands of loose stones that appear to have been used in structures of some kind. Allowing for the fact that these stones were used by Turks and other groups in more recent centuries, it is still interesting to realize that they would have been reusing stones and sites from the ancient era. There is also a paved area.

My guess is that there were inns, taverns, and apartments here during the active years of the cult of Aphrodite.

Considering the long, arduous climb up the 1500-foot mountain, visitors must have stayed overnight at this site. A worshiper would ascend to the pinnacle to make his ritual offering to Aphrodite, then return to activities with the courtesans at the site I have described. I must assume that Strabo's second-century B.C. estimate of 900 courtesans was exaggerated, but there must have been quite a large number of persons involved on Acrocorinth in his day and in the Roman revitalization of the cult during Paul's time. When the courtesans visited Corinth down below, they were recognized by their dress or perhaps by their distinctive short hair (or shaved head?), which could explain Paul's otherwise very confusing remarks in 1 Corinthians 11:2-16.

Other gods besides Apollo, Helios, and Aphrodite were worshiped in Corinth. Naturally Poseidon, the god of the sea, had at least one shrine there to be visited by seafarers coming in from a long voyage or preparing to embark on a new one.

Among the many "mystery cults" that engaged people in secret rituals and in the exercise of "spiritual gifts" like prophecy, necromancy (communicating with the dead), spiritual healing, and spirit-possession, the most prominent in Corinth was the cult of Dionysus. Dionysus, sometimes called Bacchus in Roman cities, was the god of ecstasy. The mystery cult in which Dionysus was worshiped in Corinth was made up of women. Their most famous ritual was a late-night activity in which they wound through the streets drinking, dancing, and singing and then roamed the countryside until they reached a state of altered consciousness. In this ecstatic state they searched for a male animal such as a sheep or goat or even an ox (and some say even an occasional male human!). The captured animal was torn into bloody pieces of flesh to be distributed among the worshipers and consumed as a means of participating in the life of Dionysus by "eating his flesh and drinking his blood." This was the most bizarre of several acts of worship done as means of reaching beyond ordinary consciousness to enter the world of the gods.

PAUL'S ARRIVAL IN CORINTH

• Using the maps on pages 12 and 13, locate Achaia, Corinth, and the roads to Lechaeon and Cenchreae. What did Paul find in Corinth concerning the population make-up of the city? trade? culture?
• To what city in your acquaintance might Corinth compare?
• What challenges, do you think, did Paul encounter because of the cosmopolitan nature of the city?

Paul's Congregation in Corinth
Read Acts 18:1-11

Paul arrived in Corinth from Athens in A.D. 50 . He discovered two persons there who may have already become Christians. Aquila and Priscilla (also known as Prisca), husband and wife, had been among those in the Jewish community in Rome who heard the Christian gospel preached by missionaries from the mother church in Jerusalem. Aquila and Priscilla were successful entrepreneurs in the business of tentmaking. Since tents were widely utilized by travelers such as soldiers, merchants, and other persons with mobile lifestyles, making and repairing tents was a flourishing enterprise. Aquila and Priscilla seem to have had workshops and sales offices at various times in three great cities: Rome, Corinth, and Ephesus.

Paul, a tentmaker by trade, went to Aquila and

Priscilla's shop in Corinth seeking employment. They hired him and invited him to live in their home while he developed a Christian congregation in Corinth. Aquila and Priscilla became invaluable to Paul's work, not only in Corinth but also in Ephesus and in Rome.

During his first few weeks in Corinth, Paul attended the meetings of the Corinthian Jews in their synagogue. He began to make known to them his conviction that Jesus of Nazareth was the Messiah spoken of by the Jewish prophets. The Corinthian Jews were not convinced. In fact, they found what Paul said to be offensive and became hostile toward him. When they denied him further opportunity to teach in the synagogue, a man named Titius Justus, who lived next door, offered Paul the use of his house as a meeting place for those who wanted to hear more of Paul's message. Titius Justus was a respected man in the community. Although not a Jew, he was a "god-fearer" or "worshiper of God," which meant that he admired the faith of the Jews and often attended synagogue meetings and activities.

When the gatherings led by Paul moved to the home of Titius Justus, the audience was broadened to include many non-Jews as well as those Jews from the synagogue who wanted to hear more of Paul's message. It seems that one of the first Corinthians to declare himself a believer in Jesus as the Christ was Crispus, a former president of the synagogue!

Paul was soon joined by Silas and Timothy, two of his young assistants. They had been wrapping up procedural details in the churches Paul had established in Macedonia in towns such as Thessalonica, Philippi, and Beroea. Living in the home of Priscilla and Aquila, meeting daily with interested Jews and Gentiles in the home of Titius Justus, assisted by Silas and Timothy, Paul gave shape to an emerging church in Corinth. Although there was fierce opposition from the synagogue next door, others of that synagogue joined the Christian movement. Even the current president, Sosthenes, seems to have joined Paul's congregation; and he received a severe physical beating from his own constituency for doing so. This same Sosthenes was with Paul later in Ephesus when Paul wrote a letter to the Corinthians (1 Corinthians 1:1).

Most of the members of the Corinthian church were probably not Jews. The congregation reflected the diverse population of the city itself. All kinds of nationalities, cultures, and backgrounds were represented. Some of the people were nonreligious before joining the Christian movement; others were worshipers of various pagan gods; still others were participants in local cults that practiced strange rituals and exercised spiritual gifts. The church was largely populated by working class people and merchants. Not many of the early Christians there were educated or sophisticated. Corinth was not a philosophy center like some other Greek cities. Converts responded enthusiastically to their new religious identity, but they did not always immediately grasp its deeper theological implications. New members were exposed to many different lifestyles and tended to "live and let live" with regard to personal moral standards. Some converts were rich, and others were poor (1 Corinthians 11:20-22). Various social statuses and positions were represented (1 Corinthians 1:26).

The church in Corinth was made up of several "house churches." There were perhaps three-to-five house churches with some ten-to-fifty participants each, for a total of about two hundred-to-three hundred participants during Paul's work in Corinth. There was Titius Justus' house church

(Acts 18:7); Prisca (Priscilla) and Aquila's house church (Romans 16:3-5); and a group near the port of Cenchreae, perhaps led by a woman named Phoebe (Romans 16:1).

From the greeting section of Paul's letter to the Romans (Chapter 16), we can make several observations about the Corinthian church. Phoebe, a woman, is referred to as "a deacon"; and she has been designated by Paul to be the bearer of the letter. She is to deliver it to Rome, present it on behalf of Paul, and presumably represent Paul in its interpretation. She is to be accompanied on the long and hazardous trip by a contingent of at least twenty-seven persons, at least eight of whom are women.

We also learn from Romans 16 that the house churches periodically met together in the home of Gaius, whose residence must have had a large interior courtyard to accommodate what Paul referred to as "the whole church" (16:23). Since Quartus and Erastus are mentioned in the same sentence with Gaius, it is reasonable to assume that each of them also hosted a house church. Quartus is given special recognition as "our brother." Paul refers to Erastus as "the city treasurer," identifying him with an inscription found on one of the excavated streets of Corinth that says that Erastus, City Treasurer, personally financed the paving of that street. The inscription on "Erastus Street" comes from the mid-first century A.D., which was the time of Paul's activities in Corinth.

Paul's penchant for social orderliness was severely jolted by the general rowdiness and noisy clangor of daily life in Corinth. It is no wonder that Corinth proved to be his most problem-laden congregation. The church of our own day can be grateful for this, however. Paul had to write many letters to that congregation to address specific problems, many of which parallel some of the problems of our own churches.

PAUL'S CONGREGATION IN CORINTH

• Read Acts 17–18, a more extensive record of Paul's travels in Athens and Corinth in the province of Achaia. What was the religious composition of those cities? • Who were the main gods of those who were not Jewish? • What was the importance of these gods to the people and how were they worshiped? • How were these religions different from the Christianity Paul introduced to the Corinthians? • Paul encountered resistance to his message in the synagogue. What did he do? • Have you ever tried to witness to your faith and met resistance? • If so, what did you do?

Paul's Letters to Corinth

When Paul left Corinth in A.D. 51 after spending eighteen months there, he traveled across the Aegean Sea to Ephesus. Ephesus was a kind of "field headquarters" for his missionary activities. From there he made forays into new territories and established congregations in nearby towns. He left assistants such as Timothy, Titus, and Silas to develop the local leadership and congregational life in these churches while he himself returned again and again to Ephesus, the capital of the Roman province of Asia.

Paul pioneered a unique form of leadership during his ministry in Ephesus: leadership by letter. He received reports from his assistants and from members of his congregations, and he wrote letters to several churches to be read in public gatherings. Paul's letters addressed specific needs and problems that had been brought to his attention. He wrote such letters from Ephesus to the Thessalonians and to the Corinthians. The letters to the Galatians, the Philippians, the Colossians, and Philemon may also have been written from Ephesus.

The First Letter to Corinth
Read 1 Corinthians 5:9-13

We do not know how many letters Paul wrote to Corinth. At least three of them, and probably portions of five or six, are found in our New Testament in the collections called First Corinthians and Second Corinthians.

As far as we know, Paul's first letter to Corinth was the one referred to in 1 Corinthians 5:9. No copy of this letter is available to us today. We can only guess some of its contents from what Paul says about it in this passage. Whatever else it may have contained, a portion of the letter advised the Corinthians to deal with the moral laxness in their society by demanding that the members of the church adopt certain standards. Apparently the Corinthians judged Paul's demands to be unrealistic and impractical. They felt that in a pluralistic society such an approach could lead only to irrelevance and sectarian separatism.

In his reference in 1 Corinthians 5 to the former letter, Paul explains that he did not call for separatism but for moral seriousness and strong personal commitment within the church fellowship. The Christians should pledge themselves to be examples and role models for people outside the church, and they should have high expectations of one another in this respect.

This is as much as we can say about Paul's "first letter." Apparently it had been poorly received and misunderstood by the Corinthians. Perhaps this is why no copy of the first letter was preserved.

THE FIRST LETTER TO CORINTH

• What does this section suggest about the moral climate of the congregation? • What would happen if we completely shunned a Christian who was "sexually immoral or greedy, or is an idolater, reviler, drunkard, or robber" (1 Corinthians 5:11)?

• Is it our Christian aim to "drive out the wicked person from among you" (5:13), to drive out wickedness, or both?
• How as a Christian community do we deal with sin?
• Imagine being a part of a new Christian church without having the benefit and guidance of the New Testament, only the Hebrew Scriptures and the oral teachings about Jesus from the apostles. How would Paul's letters have been received by your group? • On what basis would you grant or deny Paul's authority to tell you what it means to be a Christian? • What does it mean to your understanding of the Bible that Paul seems to have written other letters to Corinth that are not included in our New Testament? • How do you feel about the fact that what we have in First and Second Corinthians seems to be portions of several different letters?

The Second Letter to Corinth
Read 1 Corinthians 1:1-3, 10-12; 7:1; 16:15-18

Paul's "second letter" was the very lengthy one that we have in our New Testament as First Corinthians. Many things had happened in Corinth since Paul left there. Visits to Ephesus by "Chloe's people" (1 Corinthians 1:11) and by "Stephanas, Fortunatus, and Achaicus" (16:17) made Paul aware of very disturbing problems in the church fellowship. Several of these problems were listed and described in a letter to Paul from Corinthian leaders with an urgent request for advice and guidance (7:1). This letter may have been delivered to Paul by the three visitors mentioned in 16:15-18. If so, the same visitors would have taken Paul's "second letter" (which is our First Corinthians) back to Corinth with them.

Writing from Ephesus, Paul first dealt with the factionalism that threatened to destroy the Christian movement in Corinth. He called upon those who were proclaiming loyalty to him to join with those who looked to Apollos as their spiritual leader and with other groups to become one united community. Paul then addressed each of the issues listed in their letter to him, usually introducing each issue with the words, "now concerning" (7:1, 25; 8:1; 12:1).

THE SECOND LETTER TO CORINTH

• Paul is very concerned for proper harmony in the church. What form has the disharmony taken? • How does Paul address it? • How do we handle factionalism, cliques, and power issues in the church today? • What do you do to promote harmony in your own Christian community?

The Third Letter to Corinth
Read 2 Corinthians 10:1-2; 13:10

Paul's "second letter," the one we have in our New Testament as First Corinthians, was no better received than the first letter had been. There was criticism of Paul by many in the congregation. They made fun of his "leadership by letter," saying that he was bold in writing but meek in person. They laughed at his conservative views on moral issues, calling him naive and inexperienced in the ways of the world.

Paul's "third letter," sometimes referred to as "the angry letter," may possibly be found in our New Testament as Chapters 10–13 of Second Corinthians. Obviously he was very upset when he wrote. He was stung by the criticisms and angered by the ridicule. Paul threatened that he would be firm and severe with wrongdoers and detractors on his next visit to Corinth. He dictated the letter hastily and sent Titus directly across the Aegean Sea with instructions to deliver it forcefully in a gathering of the Corinthian Christians.

THE THIRD LETTER TO CORINTH

• How was Paul attempting to uphold this congregation? • Is it ever right to challenge the leaders of the church, even if they have as fine a "resumé" as Paul's? • How do we identify and deal with "false teaching" in the church? with "boasting"? with "thorns in the flesh"? with disappointment and disobedience? with self-testing?

The Fourth Letter to Corinth
Read 2 Corinthians 2:1-4, 12-13; 7:5-9

As soon as Titus sailed away from Ephesus with the "third letter," Paul began to regret having written in anger. Perhaps he would have recalled Titus and the letter if he could have reached him. Paul's plan was to follow his established circuit to visit his congregations: north from Ephesus to Troas; across the sea into Macedonia to Philippi, Thessalonica, and Beroea; then south to Corinth. The journey usually took a few months, allowing for some work with each of the churches along the way. Titus was to deliver the "third letter," read it to the congregation, receive their response, and begin along the circuit in reverse to meet Paul along the way.

By the time Paul reached his first station in Troas, he was already impatient to hear from Titus. Unable to concentrate on his work in Troas, Paul pushed on across the sea. Somewhere in Macedonia he met Titus. Paul was enormously relieved to find that the Corinthians had received the angry letter well. They realized that they had deeply offended their spiritual father, and they instructed Titus to tender their sincere apology and their pledge to heed Paul's earlier advice. Paul was so relieved by this report that he immediately wrote a reply for Titus to take back by return mail.

This "fourth letter" from Paul to Corinth is found in our New Testament as portions of 2 Corinthians 1–9. These chapters are a collection of portions of several letters. Parts of Paul's "fourth letter," sometimes called "the apology letter," seem to be mixed with parts of other letters, making it difficult to identify it with precision. The reader can observe the fragmentary nature of these chapters by reading 2 Corinthians 2:12-13 and then skipping over to read 7:5-9. It appears that a portion of another letter may stand between two portions of the "fourth letter."

It is not difficult, however, to hear the profound relief expressed by Paul in the "fourth letter." In 2 Corinthians 1:3-7, he used a form of the word *console* ten times in four sentences. He described his extreme restlessness in Troas and his anxiety in Macedonia until Titus arrived at last. Paul promised to move quickly through the remaining stops on the circuit so that he could arrive in Corinth as soon as possible. He did as he promised.

After a fruitful second visit of several months in Corinth, during which he wrote the great Letter to the Romans, Paul left Greece, never to return. He sailed by Ephesus to say his farewell there before going on to Rome by way of Palestine.

THE FOURTH LETTER TO CORINTH

• Paul seems to suggest, or at least to hint, that someone had stirred up the congregation's behaviors that elicited Paul's pain and anger. He counsels repentance and forgiveness. What do you make of Paul's change in attitude? of his call for forgiveness? • What does it cost you and the community to fail to repent or to forgive? What are the blessings when you do?

IN CLOSING

• Review your learnings from the session material and from the biblical text. What are the key points? • How was the truth about Jesus Christ proclaimed? • What personal insights have you gained? • If you took very much to heart the most important point from the selected Scriptures, what would it cal you to do or to be?

• Consider your relationship to Jesus Christ and to the church and take some time in prayer to make or renew your commitment. • Close with sentence prayers for Christian unity in the church.

II PAUL'S METHOD FOR MAKING MORAL DECISIONS

Morality and Pluralism

In an extremely pluralistic society, moral decisions are difficult to make; and once made, they are difficult to maintain when equally sincere people disagree with one another on specific issues. When values are defined differently by competing groups and when the authority to speak the final word is given to the individual conscience, the absolute quality of moral standards can easily give way to relativism: "It may be wrong for you, but it is not wrong for me." This kind of pluralism reduces moral imperatives to personal opinions and preferences.

Corinth was a pluralistic society. Many nationalities and cultural backgrounds were brought together by the Emperor Julius Caesar in 44 B.C. to form a Roman city on the ruins of the old Greek city. Because of the strategic location of Corinth, much of the maritime traffic in the Mediterranean passed through, bringing new and different customs and behaviors. There were almost one hundred religious groups in Corinth at the time of Paul, each one offering its own interpretation of values and morality.

Paul came to Corinth out of a Jewish cultural background that provided clear and definite moral standards. Jewish attitudes about sexual practices, family life, personal hygiene, and pietistic restraints on behavior were part of Paul's cultural heritage and his more particular background as a Pharisee. As founder and leader of the church in Corinth, Paul felt an obligation to pursue a moral consensus for the Christian community without imposing the full measure of his own heritage on persons from other backgrounds.

The cultural context of Paul's Corinth was in many ways similar to that in which the Christian church must function in the contemporary world. Like Paul in Corinth, if the church today simply asserts its traditional position on a moral issue without addressing differences raised by pluralism, it makes itself irrelevant, nothing more than another special interest group. How can the church witness to strong and meaningful moral principles and moral behavior in the context of a pluralistic society? As we examine Paul's method of responding to the situation in Corinth, perhaps we can gain some insights for forging a viable moral stance in our own society.

MORALITY AND PLURALISM

• Review the differences in moral attitudes and behavior between Jewish and Gentile Christians. What are your initial thoughts about whether the church can witness to strong and meaningful moral principles and moral behavior in the context of a pluralistic society?

The Church Is a Moral Community
Read 1 Corinthians 5:1-13; 6:9-10

Paul observed in Corinthian society an alarming amount of behavior that he considered to be irresponsible and degenerate. He provided several lists of unacceptable behavior, such as the one in 1 Corinthians 6:9-10: "Fornicators, idolaters, adulterers, male prostitutes, sodomites, thieves, the greedy, drunkards, revilers, robbers—none of these will inherit the kingdom of God." Paul felt the Christian community must set a high moral example. It was imperative that Christians double their efforts to exhibit restraint and discipline in their own lives. There should be a moral quality to their community that could be admired and emulated by the rest of society.

Apparently Paul had written an earlier letter to the Corinthian Christians urging this calling upon them (1 Corinthians 5:9). They seem to have dismissed his admonition as the naive babbling of a man who did not appreciate the nature of a pluralistic society. Paul explained that he meant that Christians should shun association with immoral persons within the church fellowship: "I wrote to you in my letter not to associate with sexually immoral persons—not at all meaning the immoral of this world, or the greedy and robbers, or idolaters, since you would then need to go out of the world. But now I am writing to you not to associate with anyone who bears the name of brother or sister who is sexually immoral or greedy, or is an idolater, reviler, drunkard, or robber. Do not even eat with such a one" (5:9-11).

Paul was very upset about a situation in the church community that seemed to him to set exactly the wrong example for the rest of society. "A man is living with his father's wife," said Paul (1 Corinthians 5:1). This could be a script for a soap opera! One can imagine a widower marrying a woman about the age of his own son and a love affair developing behind the old man's back in his own household. What really upset Paul was the arrogance of the Christian community toward the situation (5:2). The Christians adopted the same attitude of tolerance that was characteristic of Corinthian society in general where each person's moral behavior was no one's business but his or her own. Not in the church community, said Paul! It is our responsibility to set a higher standard; to exemplify a better way; to lead the larger community out of its destructive, sinful patterns of behavior. Therefore, those persons who refused to commit themselves to high morals were not to be counted as members of the church fellowship. They were to be "hand[ed] over to Satan" (5:5), meaning they were to be denied the supportive fellowship of the Christian community. "Do not even eat with such a one" (5:11) probably means do not allow them to share in the community meal that preceded the celebration of the Lord's Supper.

Is this good advice for the church in our day? Certainly a policy of exclusion can lead to hypocrisy, judgmentalism, and other characteristics that move in the opposite direction from the Jesus who ate with sinners and associated with the outcasts among his neighbors.

We must avoid making a general rule for all churches out of an attempt by Paul to deal with special circumstances in Corinth. It is possible that even in Corinth such a policy was carried too far, and Paul was forced to modify it. In 2 Corinthians 2:5-11, Paul advised the Corinthian church to ease up on its punishment of one of its members. You have confronted him with the error of his ways, said Paul; now you should give him your forgiveness and encouragement. "So I urge you to reaffirm your love for him," he said (2 Corinthians 2:8).

The important lesson to learn from this situation is that the church must strive for a higher morality that will set an example for a pluralistic society suffering from moral confusion. We cannot exempt ourselves from the confusion, but we can in the midst of it make our own commitments and live by them. Paul challenges the church in another letter, "I appeal to you therefore, brothers and sisters, by the mercies of God, to present your bodies as a living sacrifice, holy and acceptable to God, which is your spiritual worship. Do not be conformed to this world, but be transformed by the renewing of your minds, so that you may discern what is the will of God—what is good and acceptable and perfect" (Romans 12:1-2).

THE CHURCH IS A MORAL COMMUNITY

• Does our own list of societal taboos match Paul's list in 5:9-11 and 6:9-10? • How do we set standards for acceptable and unacceptable behavior? • Does time change our attitude about such behaviors? Should it? • Where do you draw the line between what you consider moral and immoral behavior? • When, if ever, do exceptions justify modifying a rule? When are people more (or less) important than moral codes?

The Human Body Is the Temple of the Holy Spirit
Read 1 Corinthians 6:12-20; 9:24-27

It was to the church at Corinth that Paul first presented the metaphor of the church as the body of Christ. He saw the individual members of the church as the embodiment of Christ himself. The Holy Spirit of God that dwelt in Jesus now lived in them. Their bodies had become God's "temples," replacing the temples of stone in which other gods were glorified. The Corinthian Christians were the channels through whom God became present and active in the daily life of Corinthian society.

This concept called for special moral purity on the part of the Christians. They were to refrain from some of the activities around them, such as the patronizing of the many prostitutes who were so readily available. With the Temple of Aphrodite lending religious endorsement and an aura of acceptability to having sex with prostitutes, Paul had to push hard to make a case for abstinence.

Most versions of Greek and Roman religions separated the soul from the body and claimed that bodily pursuits were meaningless. What happened to the body was not important, and therefore personal moral purity was not a very important concept. Paul himself came out of a tradition that did not distinguish between "soul" and "body" but rather saw body and soul as a single entity. When he added to this the idea that God's Spirit lives in the world through the bodily existence of Christians, he made a strong case for the necessity of moral purity. To defile your own body was to defile Christ himself.

How could Paul make this point clear and vivid for the Corinthians? He saw all around him in Corinth a great admiration for athletic prowess. The Isthmian Games, parallel to the Olympic Games in the sister city of Olympia, were held periodically in Corinth. The Corinthians were proud of their city being the site for the games; the people treated the international competitors who came there as celebrities and heroes. Paul saw in this an opportunity to make his point about respect for the human body.

He spoke of how racing and boxing required careful training, discipline, and restraint (1 Corinthians 9:24-27). "Athletes exercise self-control in all things," he said, and then added that like athletes, "I punish my body and enslave it." Without this kind of rigorous training, athletes would find themselves "disqualified," declared unfit to compete for the prize. The same is true, said Paul, of Christians. If they overindulge their bodies, if they shun the sacrifices of a self-disciplined life, they will become disqualified as members of the body of Christ. They will not be taken seriously as participants in the Christ event. Paul was bold enough to call Christians to self-restraint and even to self-sacrifice in a self-indulgent society.

Modern American culture has enormous respect for athletic prowess. Professional athletes are among the highest paid members of our society. They are indeed treated as celebrities and heroes. They are held up as role models for children and youth. An athlete caught abusing his or her body with drugs or engaging in other types of unhealthy behavior invites disgrace.

Some modern Americans are almost cultic in their commitment to a healthy body. Running, body building, swimming, golfing, and other participation sports have never been more popular. Health food stores and shops specializing in clothing and equipment for outdoor activities such as backpacking, rafting, and skiing are found in shopping malls everywhere. Losing weight, counting calories, and watching cholesterol levels and fat grams are frequent subjects for everyday conversation.

Such widespread concern for bodily health seems contradictory to the even more widespread forms of bodily abuse that are found in modern society. Drug abuse threatens to drown us all in a tidal wave of sleaze and crime. Loose sexual behavior has been a catalyst for the AIDS epidemic and other sexually transmitted diseases. Alcohol and tobacco addictions take an enormous yearly toll on human bodies.

So Paul's metaphor may be a helpful one for our situation. Christians should see their bodies as "temples of the Holy Spirit," physical instruments through whom God is made present in the world. As Mother Teresa lovingly caressed a diseased and suffering person, her hands became the hands of Jesus. As a Christian youth says, "No!" to the invitation to use drugs, it is the body of Christ that is kept free from contamination. As wise decisions are made about diet, exercise, and hygiene, Christ is being served. A theology of the body steers us away from both the abuse of the body and the cultic worship of the body that characterize modern society. Bodily existence is placed in proper perspective as the expression of spiritual wholeness. As you listen again to Paul's charge to the Corinthians, remember that for him "glorify" means "to make present": "Therefore glorify God in your body" (1 Corinthians 6:20).

THE HUMAN BODY IS THE TEMPLE OF THE HOLY SPIRIT

• Why was purity of body so important to Paul and such a point of resistance? • In a culture that is obsessive about both body image and personal comfort, how should we interpret the concept of the body as the Spirit's temple? • What does it mean to you to glorify God in your body? How do you do it? Is it important to you? Explain.

Responsible Freedom
Read 1 Corinthians 8:1-13; 10:23-31

Paul encountered the difficulty of establishing moral standards in a setting of cultural pluralism as he attempted to answer a specific question the Corinthian Christians addressed to him. The question was, "Is it immoral to eat meat that has been previously offered in sacrifice to idols?"

There were many religious cults in Corinth. There were small temples all over town for the worship of Apollo, Poseidon, Dionysus, and dozens of other gods and goddesses. In most of these temples, worship involved the sacrifice of birds or animals on an altar. Usually only a part of the animal was used, perhaps the liver or the heart or the intestines. Fortunately for the priests, this left most of the animal unused by the gods. The priests could then eat or sell to others the remaining parts, such as the T-bones or the ribs or the drumsticks. In fact, some of the temples had places of sacrificial worship in the front part of the building and a public meat market in the rear. It was common practice in Corinth to buy meat for the family table from priests.

This situation created a moral dilemma for all Jews, including those who had become a part of the Christian church in Corinth. The prohibition against idolatry was one of the Ten Commandments of Moses, and worshiping other gods than the one true God was strictly forbidden. It appeared to many faithful Jews that eating meat that had been associated with the worship of pagan gods was breaking the commandment by supporting the pagan system of sacrifice. They thought it was morally wrong to eat such meat.

However, many of the Corinthian Christians were not Jews and knew of no moral stricture against eating meat that had been offered in pagan sacrifices. In fact, some of the Corinthian Christians saw no harm in participating in some of the services in various temples. What could it hurt to say a prayer to Poseidon, god of the sea, before making a voyage? Why not stop in to worship the goddess of fertility when you get your crops planted? What could it hurt? And who knows, perhaps it would help.

So here we have a very specific instance of the difficulties pluralism sometimes raises. Some people thought it was perfectly all right to eat the meat that had been sacrificed to pagan gods, and other people thought doing so was morally wrong. Yet all of them were in the Christian fellowship together, and they had numerous church suppers in which they ate from one another's delicious "covered-dish" offerings. So what should they do? Forbid anyone to bring meat from a temple meat market? The ones who thought nothing was wrong with this practice said, "Why should my liberty be subject to the judgment of someone else's conscience?" (1 Corinthians 10:29).

Paul was sympathetic to those who had this attitude. They felt that the traditionalists were unenlightened and obstinate. Educated, informed people should know that there was nothing wrong with the meat and that sacrifices on pagan altars were meaningless anyway, since pagan gods were purely imaginary. The prohibitionists were being silly!

Paul was a brilliant and educated person. He was anything but a traditionalist, having declared that it was faith in God's grace rather than obedience to the moral law that would bring salvation. Paul basically agreed that there really was nothing wrong with the meat and that it could be eaten without any pangs of conscience. He did not want to place this issue on the same moral level with others that he considered to be of a more absolute nature, for example, the situation of incest mentioned above. But Paul raised another dimension of the question that did constitute an important moral issue for all Christians. He put it quite succinctly: "If food is a cause of their falling, I will never eat meat, so that I may not cause one of them to fall" (1 Corinthians 8:13).

The moral principle Paul was raising was the effect of one's actions on other persons. We do not act in a vacuum. What we decide to do affects other persons, and we have a responsibility to consider the possible consequences on the whole Christian community when we are making a decision about a moral issue.

In defense of their practice of moral liberty, the Corinthians seem to have been fond of "sloganeering." They quoted sayings from philosophers and from literature. As a part of his rhetoric to persuade the Corinthians to take their moral lives more seriously, Paul met these quotes with other quotes in a kind of "battle of wise sayings." In some cases he composed a saying to counter one of theirs. Here are some of the pairings:

The Corinthians	Paul
All things are lawful.	But not all things are beneficial, and not all things build up (10:23).
All of us possess knowledge.	Knowledge puffs up, but love builds up (8:1).
Food will not bring us close to God. We are no worse off if we do not eat, and no better off if we do.	Take care that this liberty of yours does not somehow become a stumbling block to the weak (8:8-9).
No idol in the world really exists (8:4).	It is not everyone, however, who has this knowledge (8:7).
Food is meant for the stomach and the stomach for food.	God will destroy both one and the other. The body is meant not for fornication but for the Lord and the Lord for the body (6:13).

Many of the arguments put forward by the Corinthian church seemed to be rationalizations for escaping all moral restrictions. The Corinthians wanted religious leaders to "get off their backs." They were wise in the ways of the world, enlightened, and free from inhibitions that were prescribed by tradition. Paul met such arguments by pointing to the Christian's responsibility for the well-being of other persons. Paul would not allow individual liberty to be equated with the freedom that is granted in Christ. Christians were set free from the obligations of prescribed behavior in order to gain salvation from God, but they were not free from responsibility for their neighbors and for the health and welfare of the community. Paul insisted that the possible effect of one's actions on other persons must always be a major factor in one's personal choices and decisions.

RESPONSIBLE FREEDOM

• What is the nature of the conflict over eating or not eating meat that had been offered to idols? Since the idols are just fiction, what is the harm? What issues are at "steak" here?

• Consider the notion of not causing another to fall (1 Corinthians 8:13). Why was this important to Paul? Is it still important?
• In a social climate that praises individualism and self-reliance, what weight does this concept carry? • Is the church a collection of individuals or a community of interdependent members? Which do you think it should be? • Think of an example of present-day behavior that might be analogous to the issue of meat-eating for the Corinthians, that is, something that some Christians believe is acceptable and others do not. How should this admonition not to cause others to fall apply in this case?

• Look over the list of statements in "the battle of wise sayings" above. It might appear that Paul is hedging, using "yes, but" responses that either escape moral restriction or fail to take a stand. What do you think? • How do you view the reasoning process Paul uses? • What authorities (besides the Bible) carry weight for you in making moral decisions? Explain.

A Model for Christian Morality

The contours of a model for making decisions on moral issues emerge from Paul's attempt to give guidance to the Christian conscience in pluralistic Corinth. His method can help us in our own struggle with moral issues in pluralistic modern society.

- Christians should recognize our calling to be a distinctive community that represents and exemplifies high moral principles. It is imperative that the church use the wisdom of its own tradition to develop clear commitments on confusing issues. However, it cannot simply declare traditional answers; it must reexamine tradition in the light of modern knowledge and contextual considerations. Nevertheless, moral seriousness and proven values must not be compromised.

- The individual members of the church should see their bodily existence from day-to-day as a channel through which the Holy Spirit of God can be present in the world. Choices about matters of personal behavior should be made with this concept in mind. Although an individual Christian is most assuredly an "earthen vessel" with many flaws and weaknesses, he or she is still "the temple of the Holy Spirit."

- The probable effect of our chosen actions on other persons must remain one of the major factors in our decision-making process. Although it goes against the grain in our "me-centered" society, our Christian faith requires us to put concern for others ahead of personal preference or personal pleasure when we choose what to do and what not to do with our time, resources, and energy. For example, buying a state lottery ticket now and then may not seem like a grievous sin, except that in so doing we are encouraging and supporting a gambling scheme that entraps the poor in false hopes and weakens the resolve of our community to provide responsible solutions for poverty. There is a social aspect to every seemingly personal moral decision.

The best moral maxim for Christians today is that which Paul gave to the Corinthians when he said, "so, whether you eat or drink, or whatever you do, do everything for the glory of God" (1 Corinthians 10:31).

A MODEL FOR CHRISTIAN MORALITY

• Consider each of the bulleted points on page 41. Restate the point in your own words and provide a current image or example of how that point can be fulfilled. (For example, in Point Two, one matter relating to personal or physical behavior modeling the temple is how personal negative talk or gossip denigrates, rather than builds up, oneself or another.)

GROUP STUDY ALTERNATIVE

• Invite three or four volunteers to do a "fish bowl" exercise in which they debate a moral issue of your choosing (abortion, for example). The rest of the group should silently observe both the content and the process of the interaction. After several minutes of conversation, have the observers comment on these three points: (1) What distinctively Christian principles were brought to bear on the issue? (2) What traditional values were assumed, implied, and challenged? (3) How were probable and possible consequences of solutions evaluated?

IN CLOSING

• Review your learnings from the session material and from the biblical text. What are the key points? • How was the truth about Jesus Christ proclaimed? • What personal insights have you gained? • If you took very much to heart the most important point from the selected Scriptures, what would it call you to do or to be?

• Consider your reationship to Jesus Christ and to the church and take some time in prayer to make or renew your commitment. • Close with sentence prayers for discernment about appropriate standards for faith and belief in church and society.

III THE UNIQUE CHARACTER OF CHRISTIAN UNITY

Sectarian Boasting
Read 1 Corinthians 1:10-31

It is not surprising that there were disagreements among the Corinthian Christians. Julius Caesar had created a Roman city on the ruins of the ancient Greek city just one hundred years before the time of Paul, and he had populated that city with refugees and adventurers from many cultures and backgrounds. There were dozens of active religious cults in Corinth when Paul arrived in Greece. The church itself was a mixture of people from various socioeconomic levels.

Why, then, was Paul distressed to find differences being expressed in the congregation at Corinth? He was not afraid of open discussion. He knew the value of debate to press people to clarify their views and to broaden their understanding of issues. He himself insisted, "Indeed, there have to be factions among you, for only so will it become clear who among you are genuine" (1 Corinthians 11:19).

Paul was distressed because the Corinthians had allowed their diverse perspectives to become what he called "schisms." The Greek word gets its meaning from its sound; it means tears or rips in a fabric or torn flesh in a body. Some of the groups had formed sects claiming exclusive loyalty to one leader as opposed to another and were apparently beginning to express their commitments aloud in slogans: "I belong to Paul." "I belong to Apollos." "I belong to Cephas [Peter]." "I belong to Christ."

The original experience of faith in Christ into which Paul led the Corinthians seems for some to have deteriorated into sectarianism. Such deterioration happens when the basis of one's faith shifts from a relational response to God's grace to a dogmatic defense of the salvation that one has experienced. A relational response to God tends to promote a spirit of inclusiveness. Faith is strengthened by being shared with any and all; love is enriched by being given indiscriminately to all who need it without regard for merit.

In contrast, a dogmatic definition of salvation tends toward exclusion. Doctrines become hardened into lines that divide: "We believe **this** and not **that**! If you believe **that** and not **this**, you are in error and are misrepresenting the true faith!" The gospel of free grace becomes possessed and defended with horns and teeth. Sectarianism is often related to the "guru" phenomenon, in which a revered authoritarian or charismatic leader becomes the arbiter of truth. Such a guru inevitably turns out to have feet of clay, and the experience of the cultic followers becomes one of devastating disillusionment.

Paul discouraged the move toward sectarianism in Corinth even when he himself was the one being named as "guru." He reminded the Corinthians that it was Jesus, not Paul or Apollos or Peter, who was crucified for them. Paul knew that many of the mystery cults in places like Corinth expected personal loyalty to the cult leader from those who were baptized. Therefore he tried to discourage any loyalty to him based on his baptizing activities. Paul begins to say

that he had baptized none of them. But he remembered—
or perhaps was reminded by the assistant to whom he was
dictating his letter—that he had in fact baptized several
Corinthians: Crispus, the president of the synagogue;
Gaius, in whose home Paul stayed for a time; and
Stephanas, his first convert in Achaia and the bearer of the
letter from Corinth to which he was replying (1 Corinthians 1:13-16). Not wanting to diminish his relationship with
such key persons, Paul simply emphasized that whoever
did the baptizing, loyalty was due to Christ alone.

Paul mentioned three groups besides his own that
seemed to be moving toward sectarianism: those loyal
to Apollos, those loyal to Peter, and those loyal to
Christ (1 Corinthians 1:12). Who were these leaders and
what was their presence in Corinth?

Apollos was well-known to Paul as a Christian leader in
both Corinth and Ephesus. Although the two men seem
not to have ever worked together directly, Paul described
Apollos and himself as co-laborers in God's vineyard, one
planting and another watering while God gave the growth.
Apollos was a Jew from Alexandria. He was a brilliant
philosopher and an eloquent orator. When he became convinced by Aquila and Priscilla that Jesus was the Messiah,
he began to call upon other Jews and "God-fearers" to be
baptized as a sign of repentance for sins ("John's baptism") and to renew their commitment to live by the laws
of Moses and the teachings of Jesus (see Acts 18:24-28).
Paul was pleased with the fervor and effectiveness with
which Apollos preached, first in Ephesus and then in
Corinth. Paul was concerned, however, with what he saw
as the limitations of Apollos' gospel. It was tied too closely
to Judaism and Mosaic regulations, while Paul's gospel
was more experiential and universal. Acts 19:1-7, in fact,

reports that Paul rebaptized and laid hands upon those in Ephesus who had been baptized by Apollos.

As far as we know, Peter never visited Corinth. Apparently the "I belong to Peter" group thought of Peter as the representative of Jerusalem-based Christian faith. The members of this group would have had close ties to Judaism, understood Jesus in terms of the Jewish messiah, and seriously questioned Paul's credentials as a Christian leader.

The "I belong to Christ" group may have been the opponents of the "Peter" group. Perhaps they were non-Jews who claimed direct and immediate spiritual contact with God through Christ and thought they had no need for any mediating persons or traditions. Instead of emphasizing doctrines or ideas, they prescribed a particular manner of experiencing the Holy Spirit. These people may have made up the group in Corinth who so emphasized the importance of "spiritual gifts" that it led Paul to caution them about the unity of the body of Christ (1 Corinthians 12).

So, in his letter Paul calls attention to at least three sectarian groups besides the one claiming loyalty to him ("Paul"): those who claimed to be more intelligent or wise than the others ("Apollos"); those who claimed to be more authentic than the others ("Peter"); and the gifts people who claimed to be more spiritual than the others ("Christ"). Paul did not attempt to refute the specific claims of any of these groups. Instead he attacked sectarianism, the spirit of exclusion. Against the divisive attitude that "Christ belongs to us and not to you," Paul proclaimed, "We all belong to Christ!" He recognized that these religious disagreements, as they so often do, were masking social and economic resentments and prejudices. Christians should be able to move beyond such things and find distinctions like Jew or Gentile, slave or master, and male or female giving way to a genuine sense of oneness in Christ.

Paul defined the problem caused by the schismatics as "boasting," comparing yourself to your neighbor by standards that you yourself set and therefore asserting superiority at one point or another. The sectarian spirit nurtures claims to be wiser, deeper, more biblical, more spiritual, more enlightened, more fruitful, and more sincere. It is comparison Christianity: exalting yourself by putting down others.

Paul became very agitated about the sectarian boasting in Corinth. In another letter to the Corinthians, sometimes called "Paul's Angry Letter" and found in our New Testament as 2 Corinthians 10–13, he countered their boasting by saying, in effect, "If we are to compare our records of service as grounds for boasting, let me boast a little myself and prove to you that I am a better Christian than any of you!" He then cataloged a record that no other follower of Christ could possibly match:

> Whatever anyone dares to boast of — I am speaking as a fool — I also dare to boast of that. Are they Hebrews? So am I. Are they Israelites? So am I. Are they descendants of Abraham? So am I. Are they ministers of Christ? I am talking like a madman — I am a better one: with far greater labors, far more imprisonments, with countless floggings, and often near death. Five times I have received from the Jews the forty lashes minus one. Three times I was beaten with rods. Once I received a stoning. Three times I was shipwrecked; for a night and a day I was adrift at sea; on frequent journeys, in danger from rivers, danger from bandits, danger from my own people, danger from Gentiles, danger in the city, danger in the wilderness, danger at sea, danger from false brothers and sisters; in toil and hardship, through many a sleepless night, hungry and thirsty, often without food, cold and naked. (2 Corinthians 11:21b-27)

Paul went on to describe other experiences, cataloging them as if to say, "Let's see any of you match **those** credentials!" He later regretted having engaged in such boasting and expressed his resolve never again to allow himself to be drawn into this kind of "foolishness" (2 Corinthians 12:11). He realized that he was doing the very thing he was criticizing others for doing.

Over against the boasting of a sectarian spirit, Paul placed a sense of gratitude for the gift of God's grace. He reminded the Corinthian Christians that salvation had not been awarded to them because of their virtues or because of their merits; they received it as a gift from God. Furthermore, God had chosen to give that same salvation to any and all who would accept it without regard for their virtues or their merits. Therefore, "Let the one who boasts, boast in the Lord" (1 Corinthians 1:31).

Beginning with 1 Corinthians 1:26, Paul developed this theme of boasting in the Lord around his recollection of a passage of Scripture. He had in mind Jeremiah 9:23-24: "Thus says the LORD: Do not let the wise boast in their wisdom, do not let the mighty boast in their might, do not let the wealthy boast in their wealth; but let those who boast boast in this, that they understand and know me, that I am the LORD; I act with steadfast love, justice, and righteousness in the earth, for in these things I delight, says the LORD."

Paul reiterated Jeremiah's reasons for human boasting that can lead to divisiveness: intellect, political power, and social standing. All such human arrangements were nullified as reasons for claiming superiority over others when God's grace was given freely to all alike in Jesus Christ. The fellowship of the church was the very last place where such distinctions should count for anything at all. "For all of you are one in Christ Jesus" (Galatians 3:28).

SECTARIAN BOASTING

• Evaluate the statement on page 44 that sectarianism "happens when the basis of one's faith shifts from a relational response to God's grace" and so on to the end of the paragraph. How would you state this assertion in your own words? • Do you agree or disagree with it? Explain your response.

• Use a Bible dictionary to find out more information about Apollos and Peter and their relationship to the Corinthians. Apollos, Paul, and Peter were obviously staunchly faithful Christians. What would be the danger or benefit in claiming some sense of belonging to one of them? • Name the specific loyalties or group memberships that your Christian life involves (particular leaders, traditions, denominations, congregations, or other groups). What do you gain or potentially lose from each of these loyalties? • Are there some Christian groups or leaders with whom you cannot imagine working or worshiping? If so, how does this challenge or reflect your understanding of the unity of the body of Christ?

• Look at 2 Corinthians 11:21b-27 and at Jeremiah 9:23-24. How does Paul speak about boasting? Was he boasting? • Have you ever boasted about your own religiousness or personal piety? If so, what led you to do it and what was the response? • In what different ways, subtle and not so subtle, do Christians sometimes boast about their spiritual lives? • How do we witness faithfully to the great things God has and will do in our lives without sounding like we are boasting?

Spiritual Gifts
Read 1 Corinthians 12:1-11

Three chapters (12, 13, 14) of Paul's lengthy letter concentrated his concern about sectarian divisiveness upon one particular problem: spiritual gifts. He addressed gifts of the Spirit in general and the gift of speaking in tongues in particular. Although this phenomenon may have occurred in minor ways in some of his other churches, apparently it was only in Corinth that it became a major issue. In fact, the issues surrounding speaking in tongues in the Corinthian church provide an excellent example of how enriching diversity can deteriorate into divisive boasting. Paul affirmed the diversity while condemning the boasting.

The "unknown tongues" experience may have entered the Christian context for the first time at Corinth. First Corinthians 12–14 is the only passage from Paul's letters that mentions the gift of speaking in tongues. There were similar phenomena in other early church settings, such as the Day of Pentecost as described in Acts 2. However, Pentecost was a quite different experience from that described in First Corinthians. The apostles were indeed caught up in the Spirit, but the message they spoke was heard by many diverse persons as though it were spoken in their own languages. This is not at all like what was happening in Corinth; people were speaking "heavenly" languages that could be understood only through an inspired interpreter.

Several of the Greek mystery cults practiced ecstasy as a mode of worship. "Ecstasy" means to stand aside, referring to the sense of being removed from one's own physical body to allow a god or goddess to possess and use it. Thus the person experiences a hyper-consciousness, an altered state of being for a period of time. The person supposedly participates in the life of the god or goddess.

In Greek religion, ecstasy was the usual mode for delivering oracles. The famous oracle at Delphi is a good example. After preparing herself mentally and spiritually, this female priestess placed her body in a seat suspended from a tripod over a hole in the earth. Gases, vapors, and smoke rising from the earth through the hole surrounded the priestess; and she entered a state of ecstasy. Then she spoke, sometimes in words and phrases and sometimes in unintelligible sounds that were thought to be the "unknown tongue" of the gods and goddesses dwelling on Mount Olympus. Priests of the Temple of Apollo interpreted her utterances and wrote them in the form of verses of poetry. These verses became the oracles of Delphi given in response to queries concerning such matters as whether to go to war against a certain enemy, whether to marry a certain suitor, or what to expect in the future. By entering a state of altered consciousness, the priestess supposedly became an instrument through whom a god or goddess communicated with mortals.

It was this kind of experience that Paul had in mind in 1 Corinthians 12:2-3: "You know that when you were pagans, you were enticed and led astray to idols that could not speak. Therefore I want you to understand that no one speaking by the Spirit of God ever says 'Let Jesus be cursed!' and no one can say 'Jesus is Lord' except by the Holy Spirit."

In Paul's day there were several cults in Corinth that emphasized ecstatic worship and the deliverance of oracles. Most of these cults used women as their ecstatic prophets. One such cult that had a large chapter in Corinth was the cult of Dionysus. Apparently the Corinthian chapter was made up entirely of women. Dionysus, or Bacchus as the Romans called him, was the god of ecstasy and of wine. It is quite likely that several of the women in the Corinthian Christian congregation were or had been participants in the cult of Dionysus. Probably these women were the ones who were speaking in tongues. This would explain why Paul suggested that the way to solve the problem caused by speaking in tongues was to ask the women to keep silent in church meetings and let the men do the talking (1 Corinthians 14:34-36).

Ancient Hebrew religion also had a strong tradition of spiritual ecstasy as a mode in which to discern "the word of the Lord." Bands of prophets, or "seers," were available for hire to perform their trance-inducing dances, songs, and rituals in order to "stand outside themselves" and thereby allow God to speak through them. Instances of such behavior are reported in 1 Samuel 10:9-16 and 19:18-24 and in 1 Kings 18 and 22. The prophets Elijah and Ezekiel sometimes became ecstatic in their pronouncements, and prophecy itself was considered to be a participation in a consciousness of God not available to ordinary persons. The great literary prophets, such as Jeremiah, Isaiah, Amos, and Hosea, were suspicious of the "seers." The literary prophets favored intellectual clarity and a demand for practical righteousness based upon the scriptural traditions of Mosaic faith. They recognized that a revelation from God based solely on feelings and emotional experiences was subject to self-delusion by the person receiving the revelation and to manipulation by the unscrupulous.

In keeping with the prophetic critique, Paul warned the Corinthians about confusing just any warm feeling in a religious setting with an authentic experience of God's Holy Spirit. The test is in the content of the resulting oracle: Does your religious experience lead you to be a better follower of Jesus Christ? The feeling and the content, the heart and the mind, must come together to produce a stronger and more effective discipleship. If this is the result, then your experience has a good claim to be of the Holy Spirit, for this is what the Holy Spirit is and does. The Holy Spirit is the Spirit that was in Christ, and it is always compatible with the life and teachings of Jesus. Any incompatible spirit is likely to be the result of self-induction or manipulation by others. The true Holy Spirit is the Spirit that was present in the world in Jesus Christ and that continues to be available to those who seek to know in a personal way the God revealed in him.

In summary, Paul makes several important points about speaking in tongues and other spiritual gifts:

• Not all spiritual feelings are Christian feelings, and not all inspirational experience is an experience of God's Holy Spirit. You must "test your spirits" to see whether it is God who is inspiring you, and the best test is compatibility with the life and teachings of Jesus.

• Since all true inspiration comes from God's own Spirit and since God comes to all of us in Christ without regard for status or talent, we all can receive spiritual gifts of various kinds. They are of "the same Spirit" and therefore lead to a community-building experience rather than to divisive boasting. Such gifts should nurture the community rather than disrupt it.

• Spiritual experiences should result in the "building up" of the one who is inspired and of others who benefit from the experience. This is the burden of Paul's argument in 1 Corinthians 14. He expressed his own strong preference for gifts that instruct the mind as well as stir the senses, saying that he "would rather speak five words with my mind, in order to instruct others also, than ten thousand words in a tongue" (14:19). Paul affirms the personal value of a private spiritual experience such as praying in a tongue. However, he places higher value on those spiritual gifts that can be shared for the benefit of others.

SPIRITUAL GIFTS

• What does "ecstasy" mean? • How was "ecstasy" exhibited in the array of non-Christian religions of Paul's day? • What was the impact of this kind of spiritual ecstasy on the Christian believers? • For further insight, read 1 Samuel 10:9-16 and 19:18-24 and 1 Kings 18 and 22. • What are the benefits or potential drawbacks of ecstatic experiences in the Christian life? in an individual's spiritual life?

GROUP STUDY ALTERNATIVE

• Form two teams. Ask one team to read 1 Corinthians 12:1-11, 27-31 and the other to read 1 Corinthians 14:1-33a. Have each team identify the gifts mentioned and what the benefits are of each gift. • How does one come to have these gifts? • What is said about the way the gifts are to be used? • Record on paper your responses to these questions and then come together again as a single group and compare your lists. • Ask the group members: What gifts do you think you have? • How have they been confirmed by other members of your Christian community? • How do these gifts help build up the body of Christ?

The Church as the Body of Christ
Read 1 Corinthians 12:12-27

In the Corinthian setting Paul put forth for the first time the concept that the church is the body of Christ. Taking a positive approach to diversity, he said that some of us function as hands, others as feet, and others as eyes or ears. We really need to be different in order for the body to function at its full potential. If all of us were eyes, how would the body hear or walk or talk? We cannot do what we ourselves are capable of doing in isolation from others, and others cannot be themselves without us. The church thrives on mutual appreciation of one another's gifts and graces. This is the practical dimension of Paul's metaphor.

The metaphor has a theological dimension as well: **Christ is the head of the body** (Ephesians 4:15-16). What does Paul mean? That Christ is the chief executive officer, the general of the army, the ruler? No, the creation of a hierarchy runs counter to Paul's central point, which is that we are all one and must respect and honor one another without regard for rank or status.

The word Paul used for "head" is *kephale*, which means literally the head of the physical human body. The word implies the energizing and coordinating function of the brain or the mind. If a body part is somehow prevented from receiving messages from the brain, it becomes either inactive or uncoordinated. The body falls into disorder and ineffectiveness.

This is precisely what had happened in Corinth. The parts of Christ's body were exercising their various functions in isolation from one another, and the result was disorder. Spiritual gifts given to enhance the body's effectiveness had become *schismata*, wounds in the body, tears in the flesh.

The first and most emphatic point that Paul made with his metaphor was that **"the body is one"** (1 Corinthians 12:12). Unity in the church is not a luxury but a necessity! The ecumenical spirit is the true Spirit of Christ. Where the true Spirit is at work, there is the church; where the spirit of divisiveness, competition, and rivalry prevails, the true church becomes hampered. All Christians "drink of one Spirit" (12:13) and are energized by the same "head." We belong to each other because each of us belongs to Christ.

The second and corollary point was that **"the body does not consist of one member but of many"** (1 Corinthians 12:14). Diversity is strength. Christians should not be expected to act alike or to think alike or even to live the same lifestyle. What we sometimes refer to as the "Christian way of life" is not one thing but many. The attitudes, relationships, behaviors, and goals that emerge from a faithful life with Christ will all be directed by the Head but will naturally vary from one another as much as the different parts of the body do. "Christian way of life" should be an inclusive rather than an exclusive term.

The image of the body with many parts energized and coordinated by its head shaped Paul's understanding of the sacraments. Baptism for Paul was not "John's baptism" in which sins were washed away, and it was not an initiation ceremony as in the mystery cults. It was an incorporation into the body of Christ. To use another metaphor, baptism was a kind of grafting to the living tree so that the new branch received life from the same root and therefore became one with all the other branches. To use still another metaphor, baptism was being adopted into an existing family and henceforth sharing fully in the life of that family. Baptism was being joined to Christ (Romans 7:4). "For in the one spirit we were all baptized into one body—Jews or Greeks, slaves or free—and all were made to drink of one Spirit" (1 Corinthians 12:13).

The metaphor of the church as Christ's body also shaped Paul's understanding of the Lord's Supper: "The cup of blessing that we bless, is it not a sharing in the blood of Christ? The bread that we break, is it not a sharing in the body of Christ? Because there is one bread, we who are many are one body, for we all partake of the one bread" (1 Corinthians 10:16-17).

This understanding does not carry the cannibalistic overtones of pagan rituals designed to tap into the power of the person being devoured. It seeks to enhance and express the participants' unity with all other Christians through their common experience of the Spirit of Christ. For Paul the Lord's Supper was not a reenactment of Jesus Christ's sacrifice on the cross but a *participation* in the Crucifixion. As Christ's body, we, too, are crucified for the sins of the world; and we, too, are resurrected. All this is not in imitation of Jesus Christ but in solidarity with him. Ritual in the mystery cults was imitative magic; ritual in Paul's churches was participative. Christians do not simply observe what Christ does; as his body, they join him in what he does. "I have been crucified with Christ," said Paul; "and it is no longer I who live, but it is Christ who lives in me" (Galatians 2:19-20).

This understanding lay behind Paul's peculiar statement that persons who eat and drink the Lord's Supper "without discerning the body" will profane the body of Christ and cause weakness and illness in the Christian community (1 Corinthians 11:27-30). He was thinking of the community rather than of the individual. "If one member suffers, all suffer together with it; if one member is honored, all rejoice together with it" (12:26).

There is one body;
Christ is its head;
and we are all members of it.

THE CHURCH AS THE BODY OF CHRIST

• What point does Paul make about the relationship of the faithful to one another and to Christ? • What does it mean to you personally to be a part of the body of Christ?

• If you had to choose a part of the body as an image for your place, what would it be? How does it feel to be an eye or a hand, for example, for Christ?

• How does Paul's metaphor of the body express his understanding of the Lord's Supper? • What does it mean to you that "Christ lives in you"? that taking Communion without "discerning the body" will profane the body of Christ?
• How does the method and frequency of your congregation's celebration of Communion enhance or detract from your ability to experience the unity of the body of Christ among you? • Do you ever celebrate Communion with Christians of other denominations and/or in places other than your own church building? If not, what do you think the benefits of such an experience would be?

Christian Love
Read 1 Corinthians 13

We would do well to realize that Paul's great hymn to love was written in response to the problem of sectarian boasting in Corinth. He had the speakers in tongues in mind when he wrote, "If I speak in the tongues of mortals and of angels" (1 Corinthians 13:1). He had in mind those who prided themselves on their philosophical skills or their "wisdom" when he wrote, "If I . . . understand all mysteries and all knowledge" (13:2). He had in mind the disorder and confusion caused by the *schismata* when he spoke of clanging cymbals and noisy gongs (13:2).

As an alternative to the boasting in Corinth, Paul offered "a still more excellent way" (1 Corinthians 12:31). Jesus had already declared that way to be the distinguishing mark of the Christian movement: "I give you a new commandment, that you love one another. Just as I have loved you, you also should love one another. By this everyone will know that you are my disciples, if you have love for one another" (John 13:34-35).

Christian love is unique. It is neither affection nor affinity. In fact, there are different Greek words for these feelings. The word for affection is *eros*; the word for affinity is *philos* or friend; the word Paul used here is *agape*, or outgoing, freely given goodwill. It implies a sense of connection, a recognition that life for the giver is bound up completely with life for the receiver. When agape is present, it would be unthinkable for the giver to withhold the gift. What one possesses already belongs to the other, so that caring and giving and receiving are as natural as breathing. The body would die if it ceased to love.

Agape love is the unique quality of the life of the body of Christ. It is the breathing in and breathing out of the activities of the church. Arrogance, rudeness, self-centeredness, and resentment will choke the life out of the church. Patience, kindness, and understanding open its lungs and allow it to breathe freely.

Paul used the term *love* as a synonym for the experience of the Holy Spirit, the one Spirit of God that was in Christ and that now gives the church its life. It is interesting to note that in Greek the word for "spirit" and the word for "breath" is exactly the same: *pneuma*. The life of the true church is the gift of the Spirit, and any spiritual gifts will manifest agape love.

Even though we will continue to have disagreements and debates (as we very well should have, since we are different persons with different backgrounds and views), Paul admonishes us to do away with *schismata*, wounds in the body, sectarian boasting, and to follow the more excellent way. His message can be summed up with words he wrote to the Ephesians: "Speaking the truth in love, we must grow up in every way into him who is the head, into Christ, from whom the whole body, joined and knit together by every ligament with which it is equipped, as each part is working properly, promotes the body's growth in building itself up in love" (Ephesians 4:15-16).

CHRISTIAN LOVE

• What is the difference between *filios, eros,* and *agape* love? What kind of love describes the relationship of members of the body of Christ?
• We often use 1 Corinthians 13 in weddings to exemplify the loving relationship between couples, but that was not Paul's intent. Do you still think this is a good passage for a wedding? Why or why not?

GROUP STUDY ALTERNATIVE

• Randomly poll each group member (If the group is not large, go around two or three times.) asking for a quick response to, "What do you love?" Answers will probably be disparate ("I love my wife/husband." "I love chocolate."). Use the responses to reflect on how broadly we use the term *love* and what we mean by it. • Did anyone mention loving God or Jesus Christ? If so, ask the participant to describe more fully what that means to her or him personally. • Ask other group members to share what loving God means to them. Invite everyone to commit or recommit their lives to Christ and offer prayer for all members of the body of Christ.

IV WOMEN AND MEN IN CHURCH AND SOCIETY

Paul's Liberating Gospel

The Corinthian correspondence contains several puzzling and difficult passages about men and women. Some of these passages have been used, and continue to be used today, to justify discrimination against and even abuse of women. These passages have been cited as support for the submission of women to men in marriage and for the exclusion of women from teaching and preaching offices in the church. Some would argue that we should ignore these texts because of their harmful past. But since they are an integral part of Paul's correspondence to the church at Corinth, it would be irresponsible to ignore them in this study. Nor would ignoring them help us to correct the many misunderstandings and poor interpretations that have been attached to them. So we will look at each of the difficult passages in some detail to see what can be learned and unlearned about them. It is crucial, however, that we first set them within the broader context of Paul's writing on the matter of gender; so we will take two short detours. First, we will look at an important passage from Paul's letter to the Galatians. Second, we will examine New Testament evidence for how Paul thoroughly incorporated women into the leadership cadres of his churches. Doing so will give us the back-

ground we need to look at three often troublesome passages in Paul's Corinthian correspondence.

Read Galatians 3:23-29

The apostle Paul experienced God in Christ as a liberating spirit that set people free from artificial barriers and
contrived restraints. Liberation from tradition was the
magnificent theme of the letter to the church in Galatia.
Against the pressures placed upon the Galatians by other
leaders to force them to adopt traditional practices and
social arrangements in the church, Paul declared, "There is
no longer Jew or Greek, there is no longer slave or free,
there is no longer male and female; for all of you are one in
Christ Jesus" (Galatians 3:28).

In this passage Paul claimed that the gospel of Christ
obliterated the lines along which people tended to divide
themselves from one another. He mentioned three pairs of
opposites: Jew/non-Jew, slave/free, and male/female. In
our own day we could add others, for example,
black/white, rich/poor, young/old, educated/ignorant, or
liberal/fundamentalist. There is no end to the categories we
can develop to distance ourselves from others and to
attempt to protect ourselves from real or imagined threats
from those with whom we differ.

According to Paul the obliteration of such lines in the
Christian community is a spiritual event. It does not have to
wait for the dismantling of the institutions that have
resulted from the lines of division. First we deal with our
attitudes and relationships by personally refusing to accept
the dictates of tradition. Commitment to Christ makes us
brothers and sisters, members of the same family, "Abra-
ham's offspring" (Galatians 3:29). As Paul sums it up, "for

in Christ Jesus you are all children of God through faith" (3:26).

Paul did not expect the institution of slavery, widely accepted in his day, to go away in the near future. He told Philemon, a slave owner, to treat his slave, Onesimus, as a Christian brother; and he implied that such treatment would inevitably lead Philemon to grant freedom to Onesimus. Slavery as an institution is counter to the spirit of Christ, and it will not long endure the liberating power of Christian commitment. Meanwhile, we must not wait for the historical process to be completed before we adopt as our own lifestyle a fellowship that transcends all barriers. Also, we must pray and work for the dismantling of the divisive institutions. Having experienced in Christ the spiritual reality of oneness, we look expectantly for every opportunity to translate this oneness into social institutions and community behavior. We realize that as we do so, there will be opposition to our efforts; and sometimes progress will require confrontation, struggle, and personal sacrifice.

Paul took a similar approach to the liberation of women and men from traditional patterns and expectations in church and society. He proclaimed that in the Christian faith there is no distinction between men and women, not meaning that natural differences do not exist, but that such natural differences do not produce "law" that categorizes people in a prejudicial way.

PAUL'S LIBERATING GOSPEL

• Identify the three pairs of opposites Paul uses in Galatians 3:23-29. How did these pairings reflect the social institutions of Paul's day? • What are some other contemporary pairings that distance persons from one another?

• What barriers or labels have you experienced in your life? • What labels or barriers do you use that might prevent you from being one in Christ with others?

• Explore the divisive issue of slavery in biblical times by reading the Letter to Philemon. Paul expected Philemon voluntarily to give up his legal right to deal harshly with his slave because the claims of Christian fellowship and love transcend those rights. What similar examples can you think of? • What institutional or social rights, practices, or attitudes do you think are counter to the spirit of Christ? • What can you do while waiting for these things to change? How can you, as a Christian, help effect change?

Jesus and Women

The New Testament record shows that Jesus often acted in such a way as to ignore or question traditional religious and social role assignments of women and men. This seems even more remarkable when we remember that all the writers of the New Testament record were males steeped in a patriarchal tradition. (That twelve male disciples were given special "apostolic" status in the early years of the Christian movement may be more of a function of who did the reporting than of what Jesus actually intended.) There were many women among the disciples of Jesus, such as Mary Magdalene, Salome, Mary the mother of Jesus, and others. In fact, a group of women became the first witnesses to the resurrection of Jesus when they discovered the empty tomb (Mark 16:1-8). It should be noted, however, that the report of the women was not believed or taken seriously until it had been confirmed by two of the male apostles, Peter and John (see Luke 23:55–24:12). That Jesus chose to reveal himself first to women apparently was incomprehensible to men in that society.

The story of Mary and Martha is a remarkable testimony to the liberating attitude of Jesus toward women (Luke 10:38-42). Martha was fulfilling the traditional role of the woman by serving in the kitchen while the men engaged in dialogue with Jesus in the living room. Mary joined the men rather than the women, and Jesus approved of her right to do so even when he was pressured "to put her in her place." Jesus declared that her place was a matter of her own choice ("Mary has chosen the better part" [Luke 10:42b.] and that she had as much right to traditionally masculine pursuits as anyone else.

Apparently Jesus' departure from tradition with regard to sex roles was widely recognized and talked about in the Christian movement. The Book of Acts seems careful to report that men and women alike responded positively to Jesus and that women as well as men were converted, baptized, and utilized in the leadership of the church (see Acts 1:14; 5:14; 8:3, 12; 9:2; 22:4-5).

JESUS AND WOMEN

• In addition to the women named in the section above, what other women did Jesus encounter in his ministry? What other examples can you find where Jesus challenged traditional roles of women and men?
• In what ways does your congregation follow or challenge traditional social roles for men and women within its patterns of leadership?

Women Leaders in Paul's Congregations

Several references in Paul's letters indicate that many women held important positions of leadership and service in the churches he established. Women and men seem to have served alongside each other without restriction or prejudice. Such references include the following:

- Philippians 4:2-3: Paul says of Euodia and Syntyche that "they have struggled beside me in the work of the gospel, together with Clement and the rest of my coworkers."
- Romans 16:1-6: Paul names almost thirty (The number varies, depending on how you count.) persons who have been his coworkers and are expected to be traveling to Rome together, eight of whom are women; and there is no order or rank by sex. Instead, the women occur at random in the list.
- Romans 16:1: Paul refers to Phoebe as "a deacon of the church" (not "deaconess" as in many translations, but the very same word that is translated "minister" in such passages as Colossians 1:7). Phoebe is in Cenchreae where Paul is writing, and she seems to be about to travel to Rome on church business. It may be that her business is to deliver Paul's letter and read it to the Roman congregation.
- Romans 16:3; 2 Timothy 4:19: Prisca is mentioned before her husband, Aquila, which is a departure from the normal custom of the day (but see 1 Corinthians 16:19).

We need to remember that Paul's first convert in Europe was Lydia of Thyatira. Lydia was a merchant in Philippi, which indicates that she was a progressive woman who was not confined to traditional female roles. Her conversion led to the baptism of her entire household (see Acts 16:11-15). This could mean that she was a single mother and that she had servants as well. Also, the only two converts in Athens whose names are mentioned are a man and a woman, "Dionysius the Areopagite and a woman named Damaris" (Acts 17:34). Unlike the case with Judaism and other religions of the day, converts to Christianity were counted as members either as individuals without regard to gender or as entire households in which the leading member or "head" might be either male or female.

WOMEN LEADERS IN PAUL'S CONGREGATIONS

• Using the text, the Bible, and a Bible dictionary, identify all the women mentioned in this section and find out more about them in the dictionary. • Does the extent of leadership of women in the Pauline churches surprise you in any way?

GROUP STUDY ALTERNATIVE

• Suggest that different group members each "become" one of the women mentioned above and briefly introduce themselves. Did you "meet" anyone new? • What do you think would happen to the church if no women were considered worthy or eligible for any teaching or leadership position?
• What ministries in your local church would stop or be significantly curtailed?

Equality of the Sexes in Christian Marriage
Read 1 Corinthians 7:1-16, 32-35

In 1 Corinthians 7, Paul began to respond to several questions that had been addressed to him in a letter from the Christians in Corinth. Many of those questions were about relationships between the sexes. Without making judgments about the nature or the adequacy of Paul's answers, we can observe that the remarkable form in which he structured those answers reveals a great deal about his attitude toward sexism. The rhetorical balance that Paul maintained in each of his statements appears to be deliberate and even meticulous. Surely such artistry cannot be accidental or insignificant.

Each man should have
  his own wife

and each woman her
  own husband.

The husband should give
  to his wife her conjugal
  rights,

and likewise the wife to her
  husband.

For the wife does not have
  authority over her own
  body, but the husband
  does;

likewise the husband does not
  have authority over his own
  body, but the wife does.

If any believer has a wife
  who is an unbeliever,
  and she consents to live
  with him, he should not
  divorce her.

If any woman has a husband
  who is an unbeliever;
  and he consents to live with
  her; she should not divorce
  him.

For the unbelieving husband
  is made holy through
  his wife,

and the unbelieving wife is
  made holy through her
  husband.

Wife, for all you know,
  you might save your
  husband.

Husband, for all you know,
  you might save your wife.

The unmarried man is
  anxious about the affairs
  of the Lord, how to
  please the Lord; but the
  married man is anxious
  about the affairs of the
  world, how to please
  his wife.

And the unmarried woman
  and the virgin are anxious
  about the affairs of the Lord,
  so that they may be holy in
  body and spirit; but the
  married woman is anxious
  about the affairs of the world,
  how to please her husband

It is virtually impossible to find in these passages any

indication of the husband ranking ahead of the wife or vice versa. Paul seems to have taken great care here to avoid traditional male dominance in marriage. The notion that the woman is the servant of the man, that she should fulfill his sexual needs and bow to his authority in all things, and that she should subordinate her own judgment to that of her husband's is nowhere to be found in these passages discussing Christian marriage. To the contrary, every right or privilege that is given to the man is given to the woman in precisely equal measure. It seems that Paul was still striving in Corinthians to maintain the revolutionary ethic that was his theme in Galatians. Even in the institution of Christian marriage, for Paul, "there is no longer Jew or Greek, there is no longer slave or free, there is no longer male and female; for all of you are one in Christ Jesus" (Galatians 3:28).

EQUALITY OF THE SEXES IN CHRISTIAN MARRIAGE

• Look carefully at the form of Paul's comments. What does Paul suggest is the "rank" and role of men and women in marriage? • How did that description square with the typical marital order in his day? • What does this tell you about how married men and women should or can relate today? • If you are in a committed relationship, what insight is there for you?

Veiled Women
Read 1 Corinthians 11:2-16

Compared to the passage in 1 Corinthians 7 we just looked at, the passage about veils and hairstyles is very difficult to interpret. It is obvious that some kind of distinction was being drawn in Paul's mind between men and

women. It is not at all obvious, however, that this distinction subordinated women to men in the church. In fact, the
one thing that seems to be assumed in this passage is that
women are fully participating as leaders in the worship life
of the Corinthian churches, both praying and prophesying
(11:5).

Paul's discomfort did not center upon women's participation in worship but upon the question of the wearing of
veils. Apparently women were accepting their freedom in
Christ and removing their head coverings while they
prayed and prophesied. It is impossible to reconstruct from
this text whether the custom of wearing veils came from
Judaism or from Greek culture, but it seemed to be a custom that the Christian women were challenging. Despite
Paul's conviction about there not being a distinction
between men and women in Christ, the women's decision
to remove their veils somehow blurred gender differences
in a way that made Paul uncomfortable. This passage represents his attempt to persuade the Corinthian women to
return to the custom of wearing veils, using a combination
of arguments based on hairstyles and theology.

Paul declared a strong personal preference for short
hair for men and long hair for women. He did not get his
peculiar prejudice about this from his own religious tradition, since long hair for men was not frowned upon in
Judaism or in Greek culture. But he thought it "degrad-
ing" for men to wear long hair (1 Corinthians 11:14) and
"disgraceful" for women to have short hair or shaved
heads (11:6). Could there have been some local custom
that made these practices particularly shameful or morally
objectionable? Perhaps, but since we do not know what
the problem was, we can only guess as to what that local
custom might have been. Although Paul's convictions here

are passionately held, in the end this argument based on hairstyles was not very persuasive, as Paul himself seemed to acknowledge. The section concludes with an appeal to common sense: He asked the Corinthians to "judge for themselves" by looking to "nature itself" (11:13-14)—a curious argument because "nature" allows both women and men to grow long hair.

Paul's attempt to give theological reasons for women wearing veils also became convoluted and confusing. He makes an obscure reference to angels along the way (1 Corinthians 11:10) and presents an argument that appears at first glance to make women subordinate to men. In verse 3, Paul writes, "Christ is the head of every man, and the husband is the head of his wife, and God is the head of Christ." The Greek word for "head" here (*kephale*) is not the word for "ruler" or "authority." The word means literally the head that sits on the shoulders of the body and the head from which life and direction flow to the rest of the body. The head is what coordinates and gives identity to the whole body. Thus Christ is the head of the church, and God is the head of Christ.

In this passage Paul experimented with an analogy that turned out to be a distraction, and so he later withdrew it. The analogy ran as follows: God was the head of Christ because Christ came forth from God, and Christ should therefore glorify or make present in the world the God who gave him his being. In a similar way, man was created by God and should therefore glorify or make present in the world the God who gave him his being (1 Corinthians 11:7). Still further, woman was created from man and should therefore glorify or make present in the world the man from whom her being came (11:8-10).

Paul had in mind here the Creation story wherein Eve

was created from a rib drawn out of Adam's side. But it seems that as soon as Paul stated this three-part analogy, neat as it sounded in the telling, he became displeased with it. Perhaps he realized that it was taking him off on a tangent that had nothing to do with the issue at hand, namely, deportment for Christians in a culture where dress and hair style signaled moral values. He therefore entered a parenthesis that canceled the whole analogy and any wrong implications about relative authority between the sexes that it might have suggested. Paul did so by creating another balanced set of phrases like the ones mentioned above, once again asserting the familiar theme of the mutual interdependence of men and women and together their dependence upon God:

Nevertheless, in the Lord woman is not independent of man	or man independent of woman.
For just as woman came from man,	so man comes through woman

but all things come from God (11:11-12).

It may also be helpful to remember here that Paul was dictating his letters in a day when there were no word processors or erasers. When a certain train of thought did not lead in a helpful direction, he could jump tracks but not back up. Maybe this is why the section ends, not with an argument, but with an authoritative command: "But if anyone is disposed to be contentious—we have no such custom, nor do the churches of God" (1 Corinthians 11:16).

This passage is indeed difficult to follow. Whatever it

should mean to us today, it clearly should not be used to claim the support of Paul for traditional male dominance. Women were fully participating in worship, but their removal of their veils was somehow upsetting or a cause of shame given their particular local customs. Since the wearing or not wearing of veils or having long or short hair is not a source of shame in our own culture, this passage can hardly be used as an argument that Christian women must wear hats in churches or that men should not have pony tails.

VEILED WOMEN

• What seems to be at the center of Paul's discomfort over veils and hairstyles? • How do you follow and make sense of Paul's line of reasoning? • What points in this passage help us discern how to build up the body of Christ?

Women and Spiritual Utterance
Read 1 Corinthians 14:26-36

This passage has been much misunderstood and misused in the church through the centuries. It is a mistake to take it out of its context and to use it as biblical support for the suppression of female leadership in the church at large. Everything we have seen so far in Paul's writings refutes any misogynous interpretation of this passage. We have shown how Paul took great pains to balance the relative rank of male and female and to avoid traditional role assignments when those assignments categorized women as inferior to men. Surely he did not suddenly revert to the very position from which he had departed. How, then, are we to understand this passage with its declaration that "it is shameful for a woman to speak in church" (1 Corinthians 14:35b) and its command that "as in all the churches of the saints, women should be silent in the churches" (14:33b-34a)?

Once again the specific context of the church in Corinth must condition our interpretation of the meaning of the passage and its relevance for today. The crucial point to observe is that this passage comes near the end of a long section (Chapters 12–14) in which Paul was specifically addressing the problem of disorderly speaking in tongues in the Corinthian congregation.

Some of the cultic groups, called "mystery religions" by scholars who study and describe them, practiced "spiritual gifts." Such "gifts" included necromancy (communing with the spirits of dead persons), divination (determining the divine will for decisions to be made), prophecy (seeing into the future), healing (the spiritual reversal of physical and mental ailments), and spirit possession (becoming an instrument through whose voice a god could speak or make indecipherable utterances). One of the mystery religions of the Hellenistic world at the time of Paul was the cult of Dionysus, the god of ecstasy. The women who participated in this cult engaged in several rituals designed to invoke a state of ecstasy. Wine was used to assist the process, so much so that in some places Dionysus became the god of wine and was known by the name Bacchus.

It is possible that several women who were influenced by the ecstatic worship of Dionysus became a part of the Christian church in Corinth. If so, they probably brought with them a propensity for "spiritual gifts." These women would have responded enthusiastically to the story of the "tongues of fire" and the ecstatic speech of the apostles on the Day of Pentecost. The phenomenon of "speaking in tongues" (praying or testifying in a language unknown to any human being and assumed to be the language of God) may have developed as a syncretistic combination of Pentecostal experience and the ecstatic practices of the cult of Dionysus.

Although this is speculation, whatever its origin the practice of speaking in tongues was causing serious problems in the church in Corinth. Speaking in tongues was noisy and disruptive when it occurred during meetings for worship and instruction. The inspiration of one person led to the inspiration of another until several people would be speaking at once, drowning out one another as well as the person trying to preach or teach in the service. Was this a genuine gift from God? Should it be encouraged or discouraged by church leaders? Paul attempted to deal with this problem by affirming the varieties of spiritual gifts but seeking order and consideration for other persons in the meetings of the church. In the end, love must guide all things: "If I speak in the tongues of mortals and of angels, but do not have love, I am a noisy gong or a clanging cymbal" (1 Corinthians 13:1).

With such a context in mind, particularly the suggestion that it was the women of the church who were speaking in tongues and becoming ecstatic in their worship, let us examine the passage, beginning with 14:33-34: "God is a God not of disorder but of peace . . . (women should be silent in the churches.)" The word for "be silent" (*sigato*) used by Paul here called for a voluntary restraint, just as it did in 14:28 where Paul said that when no interpreter is present in a particular service, the speakers in tongues should "be silent in church and speak to themselves and to God." The word implies, not a silence imposed by an enforcement of rules, but a voluntary silence adopted out of consideration for other persons present. What we can say at the very least about this passage is that it was not an attempt to silence women everywhere. It is possible that it was a response to the localized problem of disruptive behavior in the worship services in Corinth, disruption caused by the phenomenon of speaking in tongues being practiced mostly by a particular group in the congregation.

Paul was aware that such a solution might seem like suppressing the inspiration of the Holy Spirit. He argued in other parts of these three chapters that inspiration comes to people in many different ways and that the sharing of spiritual gifts in worship enriches us all. But, he cautioned, this must be done without rudeness or imposition or spiritual pride. Thus he concluded, "Or did the word of God originate with you? Or are you the only ones it has reached?" (1 Corinthians 14:36).

The interpretation given above leaves several things unexplained. Nowhere else in Chapters 12–14 does Paul seem to be speaking only about women being the source of these disruptions. On the contrary, he commonly addresses himself throughout to the *adelphoi*, brothers or friends (1 Corinthians 12:1; 14:6, 20)—a form of address that would have included both men and women in the church. Yet here we suddenly have an explicit and harsh restriction on women speaking in church. It is unequivocally declared that it is "shameful" for a woman to speak in a church service and that all women should keep silent in the churches. How are we to understand these statements?

First, we should place the passage in perspective by setting it alongside other passages from Paul. In 1 Corinthians 11:5, Paul said that when women preach or pray in church, they should wear a veil. Were they to preach and pray silently? There seems to be a contradiction here, and yet both of these passages occur in the very same letter. Also, we have noted above many instances of women leaders, including ministers and other officers, in Paul's congregations who could hardly carry out their work if they had to stay silent in church. Further, the major theme of Galatians, that in Christ we are to transcend categories such as Jew and Gentile, slave and free, and male and female, seems to preclude the relegation of one of those very categories to a subordinate position.

Second, we need to take note of a phenomenon that frequently occurred in the transmission of sacred texts from one generation to the next. Copies had to be made by hand, and the few that existed would be used by many different readers and speakers in the church. Often notes would be scribbled in the margins of the text, put there to remind speakers of things they wanted to say about the text or perhaps to enlarge the meaning. As a new copy was made of that particular manuscript, sometimes the copyist would incorporate some of the marginal notes into the text itself to give future readers a kind of enhanced text. Biblical scholars call this a "gloss." Well-known examples of such marginal notes making their way into the Bible we now have can be found in John 5:3-4 and in 1 John 5:7.

Third, we need to be aware that soon after Jesus and Paul and the original followers of Jesus were no longer present in the church, there was a return to a more traditional attitude about the role of men and women in church and society. Patriarchy recovered from the blow dealt it by the liberating gospel, and attempts were made to justify the restoration of male authority in the church. Generally speaking, the later in time a particular book in the New Testament was written, the more clearly this retreat into patriarchy can be seen in the text. By the time three generations passed, the church was teaching that women were to hold no positions of authority in the church, that they were to be submissive, and that their Christian calling was to bear children and live in modesty and in absolute obedience to their husbands (1 Timothy 2:11-15). After three more generations the church declared that it was God's will that, because sin entered the world through the female of the species, the clergy should remain celibate and no female could enter the ordained ministry. Such attitudes and practices were not characteristic of the ministry of Jesus and Paul and of the church of the apostles described in the Book of Acts.

With these considerations in mind, we turn again to the passage in 1 Corinthians 14. Is it possible that a gloss has occurred here and that what is now present in the text is a combination of what Paul said and what was written in the margins two generations later? Is it possible that what we now have in 14:34-35 was not originally Paul's at all? This could explain the serious contradiction between what Paul said and did earlier in his ministry with regard to women and men and what he said in this passage. It would also explain why early copies of this letter sometimes have these verses here and sometimes after verse 40. This evidence suggests that 14:34-35 is an early marginal note that was placed by later copyists in two different locations and was so assimilated into the Bible. With this in mind, perhaps what Paul originally wrote in response to the problem of disorderly speaking in tongues had nothing specifically to do with women but was actually as follows:

For God is a God not of disorder but of peace, as in all the churches of the saints. Or did the word of God originate with you? Or are you the only ones it has reached?

This reading would make perfect sense as a culmination of the discussion about disruptions in worship, would overcome the problem of the sudden appearance of women as the source of the worship disruptions, and lead naturally into the verses (1 Corinthians 14:37-40) that conclude the entire section. So whatever is made of this text, it should not be expanded into a "gag rule" against women speaking in the church. Paul's actual practice of utilizing women leaders at every level in his churches is a much better representation of his position on gender issues.

WOMEN AND SPIRITUAL UTTERANCE

• Recall from the prior session the discussion about the order and value of spiritual gifts. • They are interdependent and equal. • What conditions in the church at Corinth might have prompted Paul's qualifications about this gift? • How does Paul suggest ordering all spiritual gifts? • Explain Paul's apparently contradictory statements. • What are these arguments? • How do they help us understand this difficult passage? • What is their value in the church today? for you?

Women and Men Today

The Christian church has been on both ends and sometimes in the middle of issues pertaining to women's rights in the twentieth century. The church has historically given theological and traditional support for the restriction of women to certain social roles and for their exclusion from leadership positions. The roles of wife, mother, and home-maker have been said to be those ordained for women by God. Some theologians have claimed that sin came into the world through Eve and that women are by nature easily tempted, while men are sterner and more rational. Men should therefore be the decision makers in all important matters.

On the other hand, the church has sometimes fostered and even sponsored the liberation of women from limitations imposed upon them by systems of male dominance. The movements that have won women's suffrage and other rights have often arisen from church groups. Many church women fought hard in favor of the proposed Equal Rights Amendment to the Constitution of the United States. Feminist theologians have articulated for women and for men the aspirations of the liberation movement and have envisioned a culture where all people would be free from discrimination. Churches have also provided all-important childcare to free women for work, education, and careers.

The quality of human life is enriched by differences in gender and sexuality. But in no area of life—marriage, family, church, work, civic affairs, or any other—is male dominance to be practiced or tolerated by the church or by Christians. And, as we have seen, male dominance simply cannot be defended by the texts about women in Paul's letters to the Corinthians. On the contrary, the great Pauline theme is still appropriate: In the kingdom of God there is no longer Jew or Greek, slave or free, male or female; for we are all one in Christ Jesus.

WOMEN AND MEN TODAY

• How has the church historically understood the role and rank of women in church and society? • How does your denomination regard women and their contribution? • Are women in positions of leadership? ordained? teachers? • Who are the outstanding women of faith you have known or known about? • How have they influenced your faith?

• Think about the leaders and teachers in your own church. How do they model the love and unity of the body of Christ for you? • How do they use their spiritual gifts to build up all members of the church?

IN CLOSING

• Close with prayer. • Invite anyone who wishes to do so to make or reaffirm his or her commitment to Christ. • Pray for the church and for all its leaders.

V THE RESURRECTION AND OTHER ESSENTIALS

Basic Christian Convictions
Read 1 Corinthians 15:1-8

The Corinthian Christians believed whatever they wanted to believe. They felt free to pick and choose cafeteria-style from the gospel as it was proclaimed to them by Paul and other leaders. If there were portions of that gospel that did not sound plausible to them or that conflicted with assumptions they already held, they simply passed over those items.

Although Paul himself was a broad-minded person and a free thinker, he recognized the need to maintain the integrity of the gospel. He claimed that there were some things "of first importance" (1 Corinthians 15:3) in the Christian revelation. People should apply and interpret it in the context of their own lives, but they should not change the essentials of the message as it had been delivered to the world in Jesus Christ. In 1 Corinthians 15, Paul attempted to define the essential core that is "of first importance."

Twice Paul used the phrase "in accordance with the scriptures" (1 Corinthians 15:3, 4). Many religions have sacred writings, and what is written down tends to be a distillation of long experience by generations of people who have attempted to be faithful to that particular religion. Within these traditions, new developments are not usually a case of sheer novelty but a result of dynamic relationship to this long experience. The most "radical" (from the Latin word for "having roots") voices in any tradition are often those who call for a return to the very "roots" of that tradition: the sacred writings, the first prophets, and the early communal practices. The right to speak a new word from God has to be paid for by a deep engagement with these primary sources.

Paul insisted that he had delivered to the Corinthians, not his own bright ideas, but the revelation of Jesus Christ "in accordance with the scriptures." Paul was not a biblicist who insisted that the search for truth must always end in a quotation from Scripture; but he knew that in order to reach the treasures of true insight, we must stand on the strong backs of those who have gone before us. Therefore, one of the essentials of Christian faith and vital theology is a deep respect for Scripture and tradition. Our personal Christian faith is not made up as we go along; it is the result of what we have received from Jesus Christ himself and from the centuries of Christians before us as it is hammered out in the crucible of our own present experience. Paul said, "For I handed on to you as of first importance what I in turn had received—in accordance with the scriptures" (1 Corinthians 15:3).

But what is this received, scriptural truth of God that Paul had in mind? It is "that Christ died for our sins . . . that he was buried, and that he was raised on the third day" (1 Corinthians 15:3-4). The heart and center of the Christian faith is the paschal mystery, the events of the crucifixion and resurrection of Jesus. It is worthy of note that in all of Paul's letters there is very little reference to anything else about Jesus. Paul never described any miracle Jesus performed or any deed in his life other than his crucifixion and resurrection. The major exception is an account of the Last Supper that Paul gave in great detail in 1 Corinthians 11 to overcome confusion in Corinth caused by a misunderstanding of the meaning of the sacrament. But beyond this, Paul quoted almost none of the teachings of Jesus; and Paul said nothing about Jesus' birth or the activities of his disciples. The whole gospel, as Paul saw it, was contained in the one great event of Crucifixion/Resurrection.

Underneath the attention Paul gave to this event was a conviction of the importance of the Incarnation. John's Gospel summarized it like this: "The Word became flesh and lived among us" (John 1:14). Paul described the Incarnation magnificently in his letter to the Philippians (2:5-11). Probably quoting here from an early Christian hymn, Paul spoke of Christ as a pre-existent aspect of God's own being, who entered the world in the person of a human named Jesus, a person like any other person. After suffering the consequences of human brokenness, including death itself, Christ returned in triumph to the bosom of God to call his human brothers and sisters into the dimension of eternity. Paul proclaimed this to be the essential gospel and all else to be commentary.

As Paul continued, he talked about how Christ "died" and "was buried" (1 Corinthians 15:3-4). This is an affirmation of the authenticity of the Incarnation. Jesus was not an angel in disguise. He was really and truly a human being, with an emphasis on the "a." Jesus was not "humanity itself" in the abstract or "the" human being or "like" human beings or some kind of antiseptic illustration of humanness. He was "a" human being, subject to the limitations of a particular family, place, culture, and occupation. He was a carpenter, not a doctor or lawyer or scholar or priest. Jesus was an ordinary human being like the rest of us. He knew everything that we know—hunger, frustration, disillusionment, and disappointment as well as satisfaction, friendship, and joy. He was a real person! When they drove nails into his hands and feet and stuck a spear in his side, he died and was buried.

However, this was not the end of the Incarnation. Death was not defeat; it was victory! Jesus Christ triumphed over death; and in doing so, he triumphed over sin that besets human beings and drags us into the dust. The death and resurrection of Jesus Christ was the beginning of a new order of creation, and the gospel is the invitation to all who will to enter this new order and be reborn. We are invited to join Jesus Christ by faith, to be crucified with him and enter with him into a new existence that is not bounded by the limitations of sin and death. This is the good news that Paul proclaimed, in accordance with the Scriptures.

BASIC CHRISTIAN CONVICTIONS

- Here Paul introduces the two most important Christian convictions in the context of Scripture and tradition: the crucifixion and resurrection of Jesus and the Incarnation. What are your convictions about these central matters?
- What weight of authority does "in accordance with the Scriptures" have for your faith?
- Would Paul's understanding of this phrase mean something different for him than your understanding?
- How is this understanding of Jesus' incarnation as a real, perishable human being central to the Resurrection?

Christ's Resurrection and Our Resurrection
Read 1 Corinthians 15:12-20

Apparently there were Christians in Corinth who considered the talk about resurrection and life after death to be merely symbolic. They did not believe that there was victory over death except in an existentialist sense—that is, through courage and commitment to righteousness in our present existence that would take the sting out of death and win a kind of moral victory over the inevitable fact of the grave. They were saying that we all must die, but Christians can overcome the tendency to become morbid about death and to despair over our mortality.

Ernest Hemingway used his magnificent skills as a writer to tell stories about characters who recognized the inevitable fact of death yet found the courage to hang tough and spit in death's eye. His favorite characters were matadors and big game hunters who knew that sooner or later an opponent would snuff out their lives, yet they refused to break and run from the inevitable. They also refused to retreat into any opiate to deaden the pain and terror or to deny its reality. Hemingway viewed such things as religion and hope for life beyond the grave as opiates. One of his characters in a story called "A Clean Well-Lighted Place" prays what Hemingway sees as a courageous version of the Lord's Prayer, using the Spanish word *nada,* which means "nothing":

> Our *nada,* who art in *nada, nada* be thy name
> thy kingdom *nada* thy will be *nada* in *nada* as
> it is in *nada.* . . . Hail nothing *full of nothing,*
> nothing is with thee.[1]

Was Hemingway right? Are we Christians to be pitied for our cowardly refusal to accept the fact of death by hiding behind the pretense of life beyond the grave? This is the implication of Paul's statement, "If for this life only we have hoped in Christ, we are of all people most to be pitied" (1 Corinthians 15:19).

---

1. From "A Clean, Well-Lighted Place," by Ernest Hemingway, in *The Complete Short Stories of Ernest Hemingway* (Charles Scribner's Sons, 1987); page 291.

Paul felt that to question the historicity of the Resurrection struck at the very heart of the gospel. If we are to spiritualize or declare to be merely symbolic the talk about life after death, are we also to do the same with the resurrection of Christ? Did he actually come forth from the grave and live again? If not, then the whole Christian gospel is founded upon an illusion, said Paul. However, this is not the case, since Christ really was raised from the dead and has become the first fruits of all of us who look toward eternal life.

Traditionally, there are three lines of evidence cited to support the claim that Jesus was resurrected: the empty tomb stories, the sudden transformation of his disciples from despair to hope after the Crucifixion, and the reports of appearances of the resurrected Christ.

Interestingly, Paul never mentioned the empty tomb tradition in his writings. Perhaps he realized that it was a piece of physical evidence that could always be explained away by anyone who was inclined to doubt the Resurrection. Neither did he use the sudden transformation of the disciples after the Crucifixion as an argument to believe in the Resurrection. Paul did speak about his own transformation from being the chief prosecutor of Christians to being an apostle of Christ after an encounter with Christ; but he did so chiefly to argue his authority as an apostle, not to prove the Resurrection (see Galatians 1:11-17). For proving the truth of the Resurrection, Paul concentrated on the third type of evidence, the appearances of the resurrected Jesus.

To the Corinthians, Paul mentioned specific accounts of Jesus' post-resurrection appearances (1 Corinthians 15:5-7), as if they were generally known among Christians and could be attested to by other persons still alive at the time

Paul wrote. At least seven additional accounts that are found in Matthew, Luke, John, and Acts are not cited here. (The original version of the earliest Gospel, Mark, apparently ended with the empty tomb story at 16:8 and contained no post-resurrection appearances.) Paul then added his own vision of the resurrected Christ on the road to Damascus as still another appearance (1 Corinthians 15:8). (See Acts 9:1-22; 22:4-16; 26:9-18 for other accounts of this event.)

What about these appearances? Were they apparitions like Hamlet's ghost or Scrooge's Christmases Past, Present, and Future? Were they figments of the apostles' imagination or a lingering sense of the vivid memory of their Master even after he was taken from them? Were the encounters the apostles had the same as that of Paul on the Damascus road? Certainly there were some unusual elements in the appearances to the disciples as recounted in the four Gospels: Jesus suddenly became present in the upper room when the door was closed and bolted. He was not immediately recognized by Mary Magdalene or by the two disciples on the road to Emmaus. He ascended to heaven in a cloudy mist before the apostles in Galilee. On the other hand, the accounts claim there was a physical dimension to Jesus' resurrected body: He showed them the nail scars in his hands and feet and the wound in his side. He cooked breakfast for them on the shore of the Sea of Galilee. He broke bread with the two disciples when they reached Emmaus.

The emphasis in the Gospel accounts on the physical aspects of Jesus' body was given to establish the identity of the resurrected Jesus as the same person whom the people knew prior to the Crucifixion. "Look at my hands and my feet," he said; "see that it is I myself" (Luke 24:39).

Paul proclaimed to the Romans, "It is Christ Jesus, who died, yes, who was raised, who is at the right hand of God, who indeed intercedes for us" (Romans 8:34). If the integrity of the Resurrection is to be maintained, the very same person who lived and died and was laid in the grave must be the one who was resurrected into the glorious presence of God. The physical Jesus and the spiritual Jesus must be the same person.

The resurrection of Christ is a unique event in history. It is not like what happened to Lazarus and others whose earthly bodies were brought back to life. In their cases death was merely postponed for awhile. They were raised only to face death again at a later date. But in the resurrection of Jesus Christ a unique moment occurs. It is the creation of a new order of being. It is the power of eternal salvation for all who respond in faith. It is not a postponement of physical death but the eternal victory over life's last great enemy. This is why the resurrection of the crucified Jesus is of first importance.

Paul spoke of Christ's resurrection as "the first fruits of those who have died. . . . For as all die in Adam, so all will be made alive in Christ" (1 Corinthians 15:20, 22). Paul was quite certain that because of Jesus' resurrection, all who have faith in him will also be resurrected into the eternal life that begins now and continues without end. Paul said this in several passages, such as,

- "God raised the Lord and will also raise us by his power" (1 Corinthians 6:14).
- "The one who raised the Lord Jesus will raise us also with Jesus, and will bring us with you into his presence" (2 Corinthians 4:14).
- "For if we have been united with him in a death like his,

we will certainly be united with him in a resurrection like his" (Romans 6:5).

CHRIST'S RESURRECTION AND OUR RESURRECTION

• Ernest Hemingway thought that belief in an afterlife was an "opiate." What did he mean by that? • Can religion be used to avoid the realities of our lives? If so, how? • How might the belief in life after death positively affect the ways Christians behave?

• Identify the three lines of evidence that are traditionally cited for the Resurrection. What weight do you give each of these? • How important is it to you to have evidence of the miracles named in the Bible? • Is it important that we try to discern evidence for the Resurrection? Why or why not?

• Look at the Scriptures mentioned in this section that refer to post-resurrection appearances. Briefly, what happened during those appearances? • What was the effect on the community of faith? • What does it mean to you that the physical Jesus and the resurrected Jesus are the same? • How did Jesus' resurrection differ from other stories of people coming back to life, like Lazarus?

• What does it mean to you that Jesus rose for you? that you will be in Jesus' presence? that we will be united with him?
• Does the fact and hope of resurrection have an impact on your personal faith? If so, explain what it means to you.

Hope for Life Beyond Death

People of all generations have been preoccupied with the fact of their own mortality. Death and dying is a popular subject for literature, poetry, music, drama, and everyday conversation. We spend our lives preparing to die and wondering whether we will be ready to face death courageously when our time comes. Most religions seem compelled to include in their primary agenda some help for dealing with death and some hope for, if not surviving it, at least taking the sting out of it and depriving it of victory.

The great pyramids of Egypt testify to the hope for life after death. The powerful rulers of Egypt built elaborate palaces to live in for eternity. Their servants and their luxurious possessions were sealed inside the pyramid with them so that they could enjoy them forever. The Egyptians hoped that their separated souls could, after centuries of wandering, be reunited with their bodies. They developed a fascinating method of mummification to preserve the body for that eventual reunion.

Ancient Persian religion taught that at death the physical body disintegrated, flesh turning back to dust and blood back to water. The soul, set free from the body, found itself at the foot of a bridge across a wide, raging river. The righteous soul was met by a fragrant wind, a sleek cow, and a beautiful maiden who led it across into eternal bliss. The unrighteous soul was met by a foul wind, a gaunt cow, and a hideous hag who led it as far as the center of the bridge and there shoved it over into the raging torrent.

Later Persian religion, called Zoroastrianism, taught that at death the soul slept until a judgment day when a flood of molten lava would cover the entire earth to destroy everything evil and everyone who had given in to Satan. All souls would be awakened, the unrighteous ones to perish in the molten lava and the righteous ones to walk through it "as though it were warm milk." The lava would then cool and form a new surface for the earth, and righteous souls would be re-embodied to live as the new human race on an earth cleansed of sin and evil and death. (This Zoroastrian imagery provided the famous "lake of fire and brimstone" spoken of in the Book of Revelation in the New Testament.)

The ancient Greeks taught that the body was a shell in which the soul or the mind was imprisoned and that at death the soul escaped the body and became pure spirit. The soul was an individualized expression of the one great spirit, which is the logos or truth or reason. At death the soul reunited with the logos like a drop of water returning to the ocean from whence it had come when it was embodied as an individual. There was no survival of personal identity.

Other religions have had their peculiar myths and images to describe the nature of life after death. The ones we have mentioned were probably known to Paul and available to him as he attempted to answer the question put to him by the Corinthians, "How are the dead raised up? With what body do they come?"

HOPE FOR LIFE BEYOND DEATH

• How do/did each of the religions mentioned here conceive of life beyond death? • Do you spend time "preparing to die and wondering whether [you] will be ready to face death courageously when [your] time comes"? • Do you see remnants of these ancient understandings of death in the world today? Explain.

The Resurrection Body
Read 1 Corinthians 15:35-45, 50-57

We cannot often speak literally when discussing deep spiritual truths. We have to use the language of myth, symbol, and story. The human faculty that stretches to find the truth of God is the imagination, and it is really only by stirring the imagination that such truth can be told. For example, the Christian church chose to celebrate the resurrection of Christ in the spring of the year (for the northern hemisphere). The message of Christ's triumph over the grave fits the experience of new life budding forth from the sleep of winter.

Paul used other images to talk about our resurrection in Christ. He spoke of sleeping in the grave until we are awakened by a trumpet calling us to immortality. He spoke of a seed being buried in the ground only to die and come forth out of its grave in a body more glorious than any seed could ever be. The acorn dies to be reborn as a mighty oak tree. The grain of corn becomes in death a stalk with leaves and new ears of corn. The body of flesh, like the seed, dies and is planted in the ground only to prepare for the day when an eternal person will emerge from the grave.

All these images seek to stir the imagination to grasp the great truth of the gospel: Through faith in Christ the Christian gains access to the dimension of eternity. Death is overcome. The Christian will live forever with God and with Christ and with those others among us who enter eternity. Speaking of our relation to Adam and to Christ, Paul wrote, "Just as we have borne the image of the man of dust, we will also bear the image of the man of heaven" (1 Corinthians 15:49).

For Paul our resurrection is bound inseparably with the resurrection of Christ. We will be eternally what Christ is eternally. Just as the resurrected Jesus was the same person as the Jesus who died, although in a new body that had put on the imperishable and the immortal, so will each of us be the same person then as now, although in a new form. "Flesh and blood cannot inherit the kingdom of God" (1 Corinthians 15:50). Just as there is a physical body, there is also a spiritual body. One is of the earth and mortal; the other is of heaven and eternal.

Paul did not share the Greeks' belief in the immortality of the soul, nor did he believe in the Egyptian concept of the reuniting of the physical body with the soul. Rather, drawing from his own Jewish background, Paul affirmed that body and soul together constitute the whole human being. Christian life after death is neither the soul flying off from the body to return to an impersonal source nor a never-ending physical existence on an earth cleansed of sin. Paul believed that the eternal spiritual person will be a continuation of the same physical person who once lived on earth. It is the whole person, not the physical body, that survives the grave. The person is given a new body the shape and form of which can only be imagined by us in our mortal existence.

Paul delivered to the Corinthians—and to us—what is of "first importance" in our Christian faith: The love of God entered the world in Jesus of Nazareth, a person like us. After suffering the consequences of human brokenness, he was crucified for our sins. But he has triumphed over death and returned to the bosom of God to call you and me, his brothers and sisters, into the dimension of eternity.

THE RESURRECTION BODY

• Quickly list all the images, myths, or metaphors mentioned by Paul that refer to resurrection and the resurrection body. How do these images conform to or differ from the images you hold? • How do you understand the language of "imperishable," "immortal," "man of dust," and "man of heaven"?

• What did Paul think will happen to us when we die? • How will the faithful be "changed"? • How do you make sense of the difference between Paul's insistence that the resurrected body is a spiritual body, not a body of flesh and blood, and the Gospel accounts of Jesus' physical body after his resurrection? • At many funerals today, it is common to hear people say that their dead loved one is now in heaven. Does this attitude seem closer to the Greek view of the soul escaping the prison of the body or to the Jewish (found in Paul and in the Gospels) understanding of the bodily resurrection? How do you make sense of this distinction?

IN CLOSING

• Think back over the key concepts and beliefs discussed in this session. How do they converge to form the core of your faith? How do these beliefs make a difference in your daily life? How can your beliefs be a source of hope and help for others? What help do you need to find hope? • Close with prayer for those persons who are grieving today.

VI A Christian Approach to Charitable Giving

A Special Delegation
Read 2 Corinthians 8:16-24

Chapters 8 and 9 of Second Corinthians are tightly focused on one single subject: the offering being taken throughout Greece to be sent to the mother church in Jerusalem. Paul had received generous support for the offering from the churches in northern Greece, the region called Macedonia that included congregations in Philippi, Thessalonica, and Beroea. He was sending a delegation to southern Greece, the region called Achaia of which Corinth was the primary congregation, to receive the offering that had been accumulating for quite some time. The delegation was made up of three persons: Titus, Paul's associate who apparently had been given overall responsibility for the collection (2 Corinthians 8:16-17); an unnamed person whom Paul described as a famous preacher and perhaps the administrator who handled the practical details of transactions related to the collection (8:18-19); and another unnamed man who was probably a Corinthian from among the many persons who traveled with Paul to assist him in various ways (8:22).

Apparently Paul had received reports that the collection in Corinth had not gone well. He was sending the three-person team in advance of his own visit to give them time to encourage more generous giving before Paul himself received the final amount of the Corinthians' contribution. Paul's plan was to sail from Corinth to Jerusalem to deliver in person the full collection from all the churches in Greece.

A SPECIAL DELEGATION

• What was Paul putting in place? • Who were the delegates going to Jerusalem? • Why did Paul send them? • Read 2 Corinthians 8. What is Paul's attitude about giving?

The Collection for Jerusalem

What was the collection for the church in Jerusalem, and why was it so important to Paul? He was quite diligent in receiving and accumulating this offering in all his churches. Yet surely the plight of the poor in Jerusalem was no worse than that of the poor in many of the places where Paul collected the offerings to send to the mother church.

The earliest mention of such a collection occurs in Acts 11:29. It is reported there that the new disciples in the Gentile-dominated church in Antioch "determined that according to their ability, each would send relief to the believers living in Judea." No reason is given except the vague prediction of a prophet "that there would be a severe famine over the whole world" (11:28). No other unusual need or emergency is described. The Antioch church had just been investigated by emissaries from the Jerusalem church because of its very unusual character as a Christian group made up almost entirely of non-Jews. So it is quite likely that Paul and Barnabas suggested the offering as a visible expression of loyalty to the "mother church" whose members had been part of the original Christian movement. The offering was to be a connectional fund demonstrating the unity and solidarity of the church across the lines of Jew and Gentile.

The relationship between the predominantly Hellenistic Antiochene and Jewish Jerusalem congregations had been troubled from the start. In Acts 6:1-6, we see that complaints from Greek-speaking widows and orphans against the Hebrew-speaking leaders resulted in the naming of seven deacons to assure the fair distribution of charity. It was the Greek-speaking Christians who fled Jerusalem to escape persecution after the martyrdom of Stephen who established the Antioch church (11:19-26). Therefore it seems reasonable to speculate that the offering the Hellenists in Antioch sent for the relief of the Hebrew poor in Jerusalem was intended as an act of reconciliation.

This same collection, or a similar one, was mentioned by Paul in Galatians 2:10 as part of the agreement made at a conference in Jerusalem, probably the same Jerusalem Council described in Acts 15. Paul and Barnabas, representing the church at Antioch, met with James the brother of Jesus, the apostles, and the elders to deal with issues related to Gentile participants in the heretofore Jewish Christian movement. According to Paul's account in his letter to the Galatians, the Jerusalem leaders asked Paul to continue the collection wherever there were Gentile congregations. It may be worthy of notice that Paul's comment in Galatians 2:10, "which was actually what I *was* eager to do," could be and probably should be translated, "which was actually what I *had been* eager to do." Such a translation shifts the initiative for the continuation of the collection back to Paul where it seems to have originated. Paul and Barnabas probably brought the Antioch offering mentioned in Acts 11:29 with them to the Jerusalem Council to demonstrate the respect of the Gentiles in the Antioch church for the Jewish Christians in the Jerusalem church.

I would reach a bit further and speculate that Titus played a role in the negotiations at this point. Paul's account in Galatians describes a key role for Titus in the discussions. Titus was a Gentile Christian from Antioch. According to Paul, he was an extremely fine example of a non-Jewish believer in Jesus as the Messiah and a blameless representative of irreproachable Christian ethics. Yet Titus was uncircumcised. Paul claimed that his "test case" proved quite acceptable to the apostles and elders and that they had not felt it was necessary for Titus to be circumcised in order to be acceptable as a Christian (Galatians 2:3).

Was Titus the bearer of the collection from Antioch? I think he was, thus strengthening his role as a test case and establishing a flesh and blood symbol of the unity of Jews and Gentiles in the Christian church. According to 2 Corinthians 8:16-24, Titus was in charge of the collection for Jerusalem in Corinth. I suspect that Titus carried this responsibility in all the Pauline congregations and had done so since the first collection in Antioch and the subsequent presentation of it to the mother church at the Jerusalem Council. As a constant companion of and coworker with Paul throughout his travels, Titus would have been a symbol of what the collection expressed: solidarity of Jews and Gentiles in the church and the essential unity of the worldwide movement that had originated in Jerusalem.

Paul seems to have been remarkably dedicated to the collection in each and every congregation. He received it in Antioch (Acts 11:29), in the churches of Galatia (1 Corinthians 16:1), and in the churches of Macedonia and Achaia in Greece (Romans 15:22-29). In Galatia he institutionalized the collection by asking that systematic offerings be taken each Sunday and set aside to accumulate until Paul (or Titus?) came around again. Then Paul would prepare an appropriate letter to introduce the messenger from each congregation who would deliver the offering to the elders in Jerusalem (1 Corinthians 16:1-4).

The Greek churches adopted the Galatian system, but with some modifications to suit the character of Greek culture. They were much farther from Jerusalem, both geographically and culturally. Therefore Paul planned to gather the accumulated offerings from all the Greek churches and deliver them himself to Jerusalem. Also, the Greeks never seem to have adopted the weekly offering approach. This is why Paul had to send the three-person team to Corinth to mount a special drive (2 Corinthians 9:5).

How was the collection received by the leaders of the church in Jerusalem? There is considerable evidence to indicate coolness on their part. While Paul's account in Galatians 2 of the outcome of the Jerusalem Council names the collection as the only definite agreement made, the more detailed account of the conference given in Acts 15 never mentions the collection and describes instead an agreement upon minimum moral and ritual requirements that Gentiles must meet. Nor does Acts 15 mention Titus at all! It seems that the collection and its bearer, Titus, were Paul's proposed expression of mutual acceptance of

Jews and Gentiles in the church and that the elders in Jerusalem never accepted this particular way of expressing unity.

It is in this light that Romans 15:22-33 should be read. Paul wrote the Letter to the Romans from Corinth while waiting for Titus to complete the collection throughout Greece and deliver it to him. Paul himself would deliver the offering to Jerusalem before traveling westward to Rome and beyond to take the gospel to the ends of the earth.

THE COLLECTION FOR JERUSALEM

• Read again 2 Corinthians 8:16-24. What is the implication of Titus being the bearer of this financial gift? • Do you see any contemporary parallels for this collection? • Do you think it appropriate to ask financially modest or poor churches to support other churches? Explain.

GROUP STUDY ALTERNATIVE

• Form three small groups and assign to them different passages: Acts 11:19-30; 2 Corinthians 8:1-4; Galatians 2:1, 6-10. What do these passages say about the collection for the poor? about the relationship of Gentile Christians with Jewish Christians? • What various systems were in place to take up the collection? • Other than relief for the poor, what other issues undergirded this collection?

The Collection Reaches Jerusalem
Read Romans 15:22-33

We can observe several important things about the collection from this passage in Romans. All the churches in Macedonia and Achaia participated. Paul says, "They were pleased to do this" (Romans 15:27). But he continues, "Indeed, they owe it to them; for if the Gentiles have come to share in their spiritual blessings, they ought also to be of service to them in material things" (Acts 15:27). Here we have a clear statement of the purpose of the collection in Paul's own mind: The offering was an acknowledgement of the spiritual debt Gentiles owed to Jewish Christians as the spiritual progenitors of the gospel and the church.

Paul called the collection "a ministry to the saints" (Romans 15:25). Although it was seen as an offering for the relief of the poor, the collection's symbolic significance was that it was directed to the saints in Jerusalem. To some extent the offering might be compared to the Temple tax sent to Jerusalem by all Dispersion Jews (all those living outside their homeland) to support the one holy temple of Judaism. The tax was to equal one day's wages per year; and it was to be sent by all Jews, even those who would never be able to visit the Temple. For Paul, however, the collection was much more than an acknowledgement of spiritual indebtedness. He wanted it to symbolize and express the unity and mutual acceptance of all Christians—slave or free, Jew or Greek, male or female—as one body in Christ. It was this larger meaning that likely was never accepted by the Jerusalem church. Apparently when Paul journeyed to Jerusalem and sought out James the Lord's brother and the elders, he was not well received. (The apostles had left Jerusalem to take the gospel to other places, as the resurrected Christ had instructed them to do.) The conservative Jewish Christian congregation in Jerusalem had a kind of truce with the Jewish establishment, and Paul's presence strained that truce. He represented a Christian critique and, in some ways, an outright rejection of the institutions of traditional Judaism. The Jewish Christians in Jerusalem did not come to Paul's aid when he was arrested, beaten, imprisoned, and shipped to Rome for further trial.

What happened to the collection? Was it accepted by the Jerusalem Christians, and did they respond positively at all to this profound expression of unity? We learn nothing about this from the Book of Acts. We do not know the disposition of the offering or its effect. In the absence of comment by the Jerusalem church, we must conclude that the collection expressed the essential unity of the church for Paul and to a lesser extent for the Gentile churches under his leadership but that no such meaning was accepted by the Jewish Christian leadership in the Jerusalem church. They were left behind by their unwillingness to make significant compromises with non-Jews, and the Christian church moved rapidly toward a totally Gentile constituency.

THE COLLECTION REACHES JERUSALEM

• The Bible does not mention the response of the Jerusalem church after receiving the gift. Read Romans 15:22-33. • Paul adds another layer to the meaning of the collection: The Gentile Christians "owe it" (Romans 15:27) and were pleased to provide it. • How do you interpret the giving of an "owed" gift? • Could this, as Paul seems to suggest, cement a tenuous relationship? • Did it work, as far as the Scripture reveals it?

Principles of Good Stewardship
Read 2 Corinthians 9:1-15

Paul's immediate purpose in writing the letter found in 2 Corinthians 8 and 9 was to increase the amount of the collection received from the Corinthians. Before attempting to describe the profound Christian theology of charitable giving that Paul proclaimed in Chapter 8, I will briefly sketch some of the not so original but quite valid principles of stewardship that he put forth in Chapter 9. Many of these principles probably came from his background as a Jewish scribe in Jerusalem. There was an annual tax on all Dispersion Jews equivalent to approximately a day's wages for a laborer. This tax was to support the heavy expense of maintaining the Temple with its thousands of priests and Levites and its sacrificial worship. Since there was no practical way to enforce the collection of the Temple tax, persuasive arguments were made to encourage faithful payment.

The claim of the tithe—a tenth of one's annual income belongs to God—was the most common and perhaps the most effective argument. The tithe could be used to pay the Temple tax; to support synagogue activities; and to provide relief to orphans, widows, the ill, and the poor. It is interesting to note that Paul did not use the tithing principle in his letter to the Corinthians or in any of his other letters, perhaps because the Greeks did not have the tradition of tithing as the Jews did. However, we can identify several other principles of giving in Paul's writing.

You should follow the example of those who have given generously. Paul mentioned how the Macedonians, who were blessed with fewer material resources than the Achaians, had been extremely generous (2 Corinthians 8:1-6). Could the Achaians, traditional rivals of the Macedonians and much more able financially, do less? All fund raisers know the effectiveness of comparison giving. Category giving clubs, published lists, challenge grants, and tailored goals for groups of givers are modern variations of Paul's argument to the Corinthians.

"The one who sows sparingly will also reap sparingly, and the one who sows bountifully will also reap bountifully" (2 Corinthians 9:6). Voluntarily sharing your wealth and your strength with others brings goodwill and a spirit of mutual helpfulness. Generosity begets respect, admiration, and honor. Miserliness begets resentment and ill will.

"God loves a cheerful giver" (2 Corinthians 9:7). Charity is more than offering one's excess resources to those in need; it is a matter of the heart, a recognition of connectedness with one another. The gift should be both material and spiritual, a gift from the heart. Charity is more than a duty or a moral obligation; it is an act of caring and reaching out to others.

"God is able to provide you with every blessing in abundance, so that by always having enough of everything, you may share abundantly in every good work" (2 Corinthians 9:8). Generosity toward those in need and toward good causes never depletes a person's resources. Like the loaves and fish in the miracle performed by Jesus, there is enough for everyone and much left over when there is generous sharing. It is hoarding and clinging tenaciously to what one has that leads to shortages for whole communities. Selfishness dries up resources by taking them out of circulation, and it denies the basic principle of stewardship of that which God provides for use by all God's children.

"You will be enriched in every way for your great generosity" (2 Corinthians 9:11). The willing and cheerful giver finds deep satisfaction in the act of giving. There is also the implication that economic success comes to those who share with others and that God singles them out for further blessings.

"You glorify God by your obedience to the confession of the gospel of Christ and by the generosity of your sharing with them and with all others" (2 Corinthians 9:13). Giving is an act of worship, or at least the authentication of the sincerity of your acts of worship. It is a way of expressing your thanksgiving to God for the blessings God has provided. To refuse to be generous would be to commit the sin of ingratitude. God has given so much, even the gift of his Son! Surely you want to respond with gifts of your own that will be worthy of God's gifts to you.

PRINCIPLES OF GOOD STEWARDSHIP

- Discuss the practice of tithing. What was it used for in biblical days?
- Is tithing encouraged in your church? mentioned?
- Do you tithe? Why or why not?
- Discuss giving as an act of worship. When you give at church, do you experience it as worship? • When you pay taxes or bills or church apportionments or special offerings, do you experience that as an act of worship? Explain.

GROUP STUDY ALTERNATIVE

- Form three-to-six small groups. Ask each group to read 2 Corinthians 9:1-15, paying particular attention to one of the main points of Paul's arguments (in bold above). These motivators apparently worked for Paul. Are they still compelling today? appropriate? • How well does your church do at supporting and encouraging members to give to the poor? to the church?
- Do you believe that personal giving results in blessing (not reward) to you? If so, how have you experienced this blessing?

A Christian Theology of Charitable Giving
Read 2 Corinthians 8:1-7

In his letter to the Greeks of the south in the region called Achaia, Paul described a phenomenal occurrence among the Greeks of the north in the region called Macedonia. Many of the Christians in the churches of Philippi, Thessalonica, and Beroea were poor in terms of material resources. Apparently Paul had not pressured them to give significant offerings to the collection for the poor in Jerusalem. He may have been inclined to exempt them because of "their extreme poverty" (2 Corinthians 8:2) and perhaps to call only upon the few among them who could do so to make the offering on the others' behalf. There is the ring of astonishment to Paul's report of their response: "For, as I can testify, they voluntarily gave according to their means, and even beyond their means, begging us earnestly for the privilege of sharing in this ministry to the saints" (8:3).

The Christians of Macedonia pleaded with Paul to allow them to share out of their poverty with the Christians of Jerusalem. Paul called them wealthy, saying that "their abundant joy and their extreme poverty have overflowed in a wealth of generosity on their part" (2 Corinthians 8:2). Although he was writing this letter to encourage the Corinthians to give generously to the collection for Jerusalem, Paul was profoundly aware that something much greater than a collection for a good cause had occurred in Macedonia.

Several times in an attempt to deal with practical needs or organizational concerns, Paul discovered profound insights. He found that openness to God's guiding Spirit often led to unanticipated depths of understanding. This happened in his letter to the Galatians when his frustration with the Judaizers (those who argued that Gentiles must be circumcised and obey Moses to be Christian) led him to discover the concept of salvation by grace through faith. This also happened in his letter to the Corinthians when his attempt to deal with factionalism in the church (the "I belong to Paul, I belong to Apollos, I belong to Cephas" attitude) led him to develop the concept of the church as the body of Christ with many different parts functioning in unity. In that same letter to the Corinthians, Paul's problem with a disruptive group of people who spoke in tongues inspired the magnificent love chapter ("If I speak in the tongues of mortals and of angels, but do not have love—I am nothing" (1 Corinthians 13:1-2).

In still another letter to the Corinthians, the one we have before us now, an attempt to accomplish a practical project—the collection for Jerusalem—plunged Paul into a profound insight. He realized that Christian faith provided a unique context for charitable giving. It centered upon the concept of "grace."

The word *grace* (*charis*) derives from the same root in Greek as the word *charity*. Various meanings spin off from this root. It can mean "love" or "loving concern." It can mean "a gift" or "to give." It can mean "joy," which is properly associated with giving and receiving gifts. It can refer to spiritual gifts from God, called *charismata*, or to the gift of God's own presence in one's life, called "charisma." And it can mean "gratitude" or "thanksgiving," as in the case of the word in modern Greek for "thank you," which is *eucharisto*. The related word, *eucharistia*, "thanksgiving," is the reason we refer to the Lord's Supper as the "Eucharist." The word *eucharist* means something like, "I acknowledge receipt of a gracious act from you, and I share in the experience of grace that your act has made possible." Thus the sacrament is "eucharist," a thanksgiving for, acknowledging of, and sharing in God's gracious act.

All these meanings—love, joy, giving and receiving,

being present with one another spirit to spirit, thanksgiving—are caught up in the Christian concept of "grace" and provide the context for the uniquely Christian understanding of charity and charitable giving. The uniqueness is provided by what God has done in Christ, as Paul stated in 2 Corinthians 8:9: "For you know the generous act of our Lord Jesus Christ, that though he was rich, yet for your sakes he became poor, so that by his poverty you might become rich."

The Greek word that the NRSV translates "generous act" here is the word *charis*, which is more literally translated "grace." The concepts are interchangeable: generosity and grace. God has voluntarily surrendered a portion of his abundance to meet our need, even to the extent that God suffers great loss in the transaction.

God's gracious act is the supreme charitable gift, and it becomes the model for all charitable giving. When we give to others out of that over which we have personal control and which we can claim to be our own possessions, we are imitating God's gracious act in Jesus Christ. We are obeying the charge of Christ that we should love one another even as he has loved us (John 15:12). And that act of generosity should go beyond those in the church with us and beyond those who "deserve" our help. Paul marveled at the grace of Christ who gave himself for us "while we still were sinners," before any action at all on our part to merit his gift (Romans 5:8).

Most of us like to think of ourselves as generous persons. We willingly make sacrifices to share our resources, time, and energies with those around us, especially family members, coworkers, sisters and brothers in our religious group, and neighbors in our community. There is a sense of reciprocity about such sharing. I am able to help you in your need today; and tomorrow when I am the needy one, you will help me in return. We can lean on each other to get through times of trial.

Grace, especially grace as defined by the act of God in Christ, goes beyond reciprocity and neighborliness. We give, not merely because our hearts are moved by the needs of others, but because we are recipients of the grace of God. Gratitude—another derivative of the word *charis*—motivates us to do acts of charity toward others. If we are truly grateful in our hearts, we find ourselves unable to sit on our hands! We must do something to pass along to others this gift that we have received. "We love because he first loved us" (1 John 4:19). This is the nature of *charis*. Grace calls for action, for deeds of kindness, for acts of extraordinary generosity.

Paul connected the two events: the collection to be sent to the poor in Jerusalem and the death of Jesus Christ on the cross. The connection is *charis*. Grace motivates Christ's gift of himself, and gratitude motivates the collection for the poor. Paul called the collection "this *chariti*," this charity, this gracious act, this expression of love received and love passed on. By making this connection, Paul articulated the unique Christian dimension of charitable giving.

A CHRISTIAN THEOLOGY OF CHARITABLE GIVING

• What insight came to Paul about the effect of this collection?
• What happens when persons feel free, rather than obligated, to give?

• Discuss briefly the terms and definitions that help us understand grace. What new insight comes to you about the depth of the term?
• What does it mean to you that "God has voluntarily surrendered a portion of God's abundance to meet our need," even to the extent of suffering great loss? Do you believe this? When have you experienced such grace?

• Make a written or mental list, privately, of those persons or organizations that deserve help. Ask for responses; then discuss the notion of "deserving." How do you decide who deserves help and who does not?
• Now discuss God's gracious act as the model of all charitable giving. How do your list, your definitions of deserving, and your decision-making process compare with this model? • Are you deserving of help? of God's grace? • How does your knowledge of and appreciation for God's grace to you motivate you to acts and attitudes of grace?

IN CLOSING

• Review your learnings and insights from this session. How do they help you with your own life of discipleship and grace?
• How do they bring you closer to God and build up your relationship with the body of Christ? • What do they call you to do or to be?

• Pray for all persons who are in need of gracious help and search your heart for how God may be calling you to give.

VII RECONCILIATION IN A BROKEN WORLD

Troubled Relationships in Corinth
Read 2 Corinthians 12:11-13

Paul had a long and often stormy relationship with the Christians in Corinth. He made visits there at least twice; and with the help of assistants like Timothy, Titus, and Silas, he personally initiated several house churches in and near that city. His many letters to the Corinthian Christians show how deeply he cared for them but also how often he was hurt by their disloyalty and their personal criticisms of him in favor of other Christian leaders who presented themselves as Paul's rivals.

The short passage cited here is probably from a letter that Paul wrote in bitterness and anger. He had been maligned and perhaps even made fun of by followers of more eloquent or more attractive Christian leaders. Paul referred to them as "super-apostles" and hinted that they may have utilized their skills to gain personal advantages from the Corinthian Christians. It was as difficult then as it is today to distinguish the true evangelists from those who manipulate religious needs for their own self-glorification and benefit.

Read 2 Corinthians 11:16-29

Paul invited the Corinthians to compare the "apostolic credentials" of the "super-apostles" with his own. Some of these "super-apostles" claimed to have special letters of authority, perhaps from the Jerusalem church or from one of the Twelve, a claim they knew Paul could not make. Paul invited the Corinthians to compare a different kind of credential: how much personal suffering and sacrifice a leader has done to further the ministry of Christ. Paul's own list was indeed an impressive one: shipwreck, beatings, and every imaginable danger and hardship. It goes without saying that the "super-apostles" could not begin to match Paul.

Having written what some scholars refer to as "the angry letter" and sent it off to Corinth by Titus, Paul immediately began to worry about whether he had acted hastily. The long series of disagreements and difficulties among the Corinthian house churches had taxed his patience. The plan was that Paul would travel the circuit of churches from Ephesus north to Troas, across the Aegean Sea through northern Greece (Macedonia), and south to Corinth. Titus would travel by sea directly from Ephesus, deliver the "angry letter" to Corinth, then proceed along the circuit in reverse until he met Paul somewhere along the way. In a later letter, sometimes called "the apology letter," Paul describes his anxiety as he waited to hear the report from Titus:

> When I came to Troas to proclaim the good news of Christ, a door was opened for me in the Lord: but my mind could not rest because I did not find my brother Titus there. So I said farewell to them and went on to Macedonia. . . . For even when we came into Macedonia, our bodies had no rest, but we were afflicted in every way—disputes without and fears within. But God, who consoles the downcast, consoled us by the arrival of Titus.   (2 Corinthians 2:12-13; 7:5-6)

Fortunately for all concerned, the Corinthians received Paul's letter well. They realized that they had seriously offended their spiritual mentor and church founder. They instructed Titus to give Paul their love and to ask his forgiveness. Paul was overwhelmed with relief and joy. The crisis in their relationship was over; the process of reconciliation had begun.

This brings us to the theme of this chapter: **reconciliation**. As so often happened in Paul's letters, a specific situation in a local congregation led Paul to the brink of a major theological breakthrough. We turn now to the passage in which that breakthrough is stated so eloquently: 2 Corinthians 5:16-21.

TROUBLED RELATIONSHIPS IN CORINTH

• Paul seems to have had his feelings hurt. What is his complaint, and how does he express it? • Other than his own hurt, what significant issue is at stake here?

• What purpose does Paul's catalog of experiences serve?
• Given the state of medical science in those days, it is a miracle Paul survived any one of those dangers, much less all of them. Have you ever been in any real danger over a faith issue? • How much would you be willing to sacrifice for your faith? • Do you think God would protect you? Explain.

A Christian Point of View
Read 2 Corinthians 5:16-17

"Reality" is made up of two things: a set of circumstances and a point of view. Two persons can encounter the very same circumstance and understand and appropriate it very differently. Our attitude, ability, experience, knowledge, and personal preference can influence our perception. We evaluate and judge situations and people on the basis of the values we have adopted, even if we are not conscious of when or why those particular values became natural to us. The matter of **perspective** is crucial to our experience of life.

In the above passage Paul refers to "a human point of view." By this he means an evaluation of people and events according to a set of values that is natural to us because of the social environment in which we live. Unfortunately, those of us living in the social environment of contemporary North America are conditioned by the suspicion, prejudice, greed, self-centeredness, pride, jealousy, and lust that mark much of our world. By observing the actions of others, we can easily decide that the important things in life must be to survive, to protect our own interests against the interests of others, and to gain every possible advantage for ourselves.

How on earth did we arrive at such a negative, self-centered, destructive point of view? Paul ascribes it to the tendency to choose to create our own principles and patterns of action rather than to fulfill the magnificent potential given to us by God. (See Romans 1:28-32 for Paul's graphic description of the consequences of such a choice.)

Human beings are given freedom so that they can become **co-creators with God** by aligning our wills with the work of God in the world. We can use our creative power to fulfill God's purposes or to substitute goals and behaviors of our own devising. Pursuing the latter course is what Paul calls "disobedience," and it results in alienation from God by breaking the co-creative partnership with humans that God intends.

God does not respond to human disobedience by canceling human freedom, and God does not punish "sinners" by imposing specific penalties. To do so would be to deny the Creator's own design for human creativity. The punishment comes naturally in the form of a fouled creation and a confused and self-destructive humanity. Disobedience has its natural consequences. For example, we can choose to neglect and abuse our own bodies by unhealthy diet, excessive use of alcohol or tobacco, lack of proper exercise, or failure to get adequate rest. These are choices that are always available to us; but choices have inevitable consequences, and we cannot expect to be exempt from the consequences that naturally accompany the choices we make.

This is true of social as well as of personal choices. We can join in the prevailing attitudes of a community that exhibits racial prejudice. We can refuse to accept responsibility for the poor and the weak. We can join in a calloused pursuit of material wealth at the expense of the environment. We should expect, however, to reap the natural consequences that accompany such behavior. We can use our ability to be co-creators with God to facilitate, enhance, and enjoy the fulfillment of God's creative activity; or we can use that same ability to break with God and create our own social environment with self-designed purposes.

Each of us is born in a world whose character reflects the consequences of many generations of human disobedience. It seems natural to us to act and think according to our experience in such a world. From time to time we become uneasy in our world and question whether there may be something better that we cannot quite define. We watch the horrors of what humans do to each other—the self-inflicted suffering, cruelty, violence, and deceit—and we ask, "Is this the way life is supposed to be? Surely there is a better way!"

Paul claimed that he and other Christians once responded to life on the basis of a human point of view, a worldly perspective. They evaluated Jesus from a human point of view and found him to be a threat to things the world held dear. On the basis of their worldly values, they gave Jesus failing marks and judged him worthy of crucifixion.

But then something happened to Paul and to other future Christians, something that replaced the human point of view with a perspective so radically different that reality itself was transformed for them. Their encounter with the living Spirit of Christ called into question their worldly perspective. The Christian point of view was so different from the human point of view that the change could only be described as "a new creation." The old creation (life viewed from a human point of view) passed away and was replaced by a new creation (life viewed from a Christ point of view as exemplified in Jesus). Actually, the creation in terms of events and situations remained the same; but since reality is made up of a perspective as well as of a set of circumstances, the change in point of view effected a "re-creation" of the world as a whole. "Everything old has passed away; see, everything has become new!" (2 Corinthians 5:17).

How can such a thing happen? What source of power is great enough to re-create the whole world?

Read 2 Corinthians 5:18-20

There is only one God who created us, and that same one must re-create us. "All this is from God" (2 Corinthians 5:18), Paul wrote. Re-creation became possible through the Christ event—that is, the life, death, and resurrection of Jesus. What is provided in Jesus Christ is **God's alternative to the world's perspective.** "Let the same mind be in you that was in Christ Jesus" (Philippians 2:5), Paul urged. When we see things and events and people as Jesus saw them, we are viewing the world through God's eyes and according to God's values and purposes. When that perspective is applied to the circumstances that we encounter in life, everything changes.

The human point of view sees competition everywhere. It fears the other person as a threat and as a competitor for possessions and territories and advantages. It believes that in order for me to gain, someone else must lose. Such an attitude fosters envy, jealousy, greed, factionalism, strife, and selfishness. It encourages fear, anxiety, and suspicion. It leads me to exploit and manipulate others to ensure the fulfillment of my own perceived needs.

God's point of view as represented in Jesus sees the world very differently. It values and searches for "love, joy, peace, patience, kindness, generosity, faithfulness, gentleness, and self-control" (Galatians 5:22-23). We would indeed have a new creation if large numbers of us responded to the events of life according to God's values! Paul had experienced the transformation that occurs when this great exchange of points of view is made in a person's life.

Since adopting God's point of view and thus bringing about a re-creation is so obviously the right thing to do, why do we not do it? We do not do it because it is very difficult to do so when we have been raised and influenced by our surroundings according to the human point of view. Everything militates against any radical change of perspective. Humanity has broken away from God by disobedience to the will and way of the Creator. This has placed us in a context of "sin" that is hostile to God and contemptuous of God's point of view.

The central claim of this great passage is that **in the Christ event the world has been reconciled to God**. "Conciliation" means the peaceful coexistence of two or more entities in harmony with one another. Conciliation was God's original intention and desire for us. But we have often chosen to develop our own desires and intentions independently from our Creator.

We are created in the image of God (Genesis 1:26). Unlike the rest of creation that obeys God perfectly because it can do no other, humans have genuine freedom of choice. Why did God put such a "wild card" in an otherwise perfectly obedient creation? The answer lies in the nature of love. Freedom is necessary for love. In order truly to love, one must be capable of not loving. Humans serve as the connecting link that enables the creation to love God as God loves the creation. Love requires risk and vulnerability to rejection by the beloved. It is an unconditional commitment. The one who loves must not determine or condition the action of the beloved but must await a free and genuine response.

The tragic truth is that we have rejected the love of God. The results have been devastating for our relationships with God, for the good creation of God, and for our relationships with one another. The chaos of sin and death is the consequence of people choosing to deny their own nature and destiny.

The theological term that is used for our condition of alienation from God and our own true potential as creatures of God is *original sin*. Each of us inherits at birth a long history of life viewed from a human point of view, and each of us accepts that perspective as the natural one for us. This is what it means to say that we are "born in sin" or that we are "sinners from birth."

Paul's understanding of the nature of sin is reflected in the Greek word he preferred to use for "sin." He had at least five words from which to choose; and even though he made use of almost all of them occasionally, he heavily favored one in particular. The word that Paul preferred was *hamartia*. It meant to miss the mark, to aim at the wrong target, to misalign yourself. It was used, for example, in the sport of archery to describe a shot that missed the designated target. For Paul, sin was misalignment, being "out of sync" with God's purposes and with one's own potential as a human person. Sin was alienation, hostility, and self-destructive behavior that ignored or denied that which is good and meaningful and truly fulfilling. Paul echoed the prophet who asked the people of his own day,

> Why do you spend your money for
> that which is not bread,
> and your labor for that which does not satisfy?
> (Isaiah 55:2)

Paul connected the reality of sin with the phenomenon of death. "The wages of sin is death" (Romans 6:23), he said. Quite often when a person who is very successful from a human point of view—wealthy, powerful, famous, envied by others—comes face to face with his or her own death, a day of reckoning is experienced. A fatal disease is discovered or a debilitating accident occurs, and suddenly the "misalignment" of life is seen clearly. Achievements, great as they may be, prove empty and unfulfilling. So little time, energy, and resources have been dedicated to the things that are now recognized as the really important ones: family, friends, helpfulness to those in need, contemplative activities that develop the mind and spirit. If only a second chance could be had, now that it is clear what the target in life is!

Do we have to wait until we are confronted with imminent death to realign ourselves? Are we forever bound to obey the dictates of a human point of view?

God has provided the remedy to this seemingly hopeless condition. God offers **reconciliation**, the recovery of the purposes of the Creator for ourselves, for humanity as a whole, and for the creation itself. By coming among us in the person of Jesus Christ and by suffering the destructive consequences of unrighteousness even to the extent of experiencing an ignoble death on the cross, God has established a new way to be human. The prototype for a meaningful human life becomes not that of Adam, but that of Jesus as "the new Adam." The power of our previous life is broken by the Christ event, and we are given an alternative to a human point of view. The possibility for reconciliation has been given by the grace and love of God.

A CHRISTIAN POINT OF VIEW

• Read 2 Corinthians 5:16-17. What does "new creation" mean here?
• As a person of faith, do you regard yourself as a new creation? How would you describe the "old creation"?
• How can we be co-creators with God? What does this mean? What doesn't it mean? • What is the consequence of disobedience? • What are some of the ways that your community exhibits this corporate "disobedience"? • What can you do about it?

• Turn to 2 Corinthians 5:18-20. Compare the "human point of view" with "God's point of view." What does "reconciliation" mean here? "conciliation"? • How does God's point of view (grace) lead you to reconciliation? • How does your freedom to love (or not love) God and others affect your faith? your life?

• Discuss the concept of original sin. What does this mean to you?
• For Paul, "sin" meant a deliberate elevation of oneself over God, thus separating from God. It was shown daily in the major and minor ways one was selfish, unloving, and so on. How does Paul's concept of *hamartia* compare to your understanding of sin? • How does "sin" lead to "death"?

GROUP STUDY ALTERNATIVE

• Invite group members to state quickly their core values. That is, what do they hold most dear, or what is the central principle by which they guide their lives? • What principles guide their decision making? • How do they regard themselves compared to others? • Ask: What is your human point of view? (Turn to Romans 1:28-32 for Paul's comment on the consequences of an entirely selfish point of view.)

The Mission of the Church

The Christians in Corinth struggled to understand the meaning and purpose of their existence as a community of believers. In his correspondence Paul gave them several metaphors for the church. The most powerful one, and the one that became the definitive image through the centuries, was the church as the "body of Christ." Paul colorfully suggested that Christians form the hands and feet and voices who embody the Spirit of Christ in the world. Paul developed this imagery in magnificent ways in Romans 12, 1 Corinthians 12, and Ephesians 4.

In the passage we are considering, Paul gave another strong metaphor for the church. He declared that as Christians, "we are ambassadors for Christ, since God is making his appeal through us" (2 Corinthians 5:20). He made the awesome claim that God "reconciled us to himself through Christ, and has given us the ministry of reconciliation" (5:18).

This became the mission of the church: to be ambassadors for Christ and to proclaim, assist, and implement the process of reconciliation. An ambassador represents the values and the cultural perspective of a society other than the one in which he or she resides. It is the task of the ambassador to advocate and embody the kingdom to which he or she truly belongs and to harmonize the natural conflicts between that kingdom and the one in which the ambassador currently resides. Paul's definition of the church's mission is clear and compelling: **to be agents of reconciliation in a broken world**.

The need for such agents in the modern world seems to grow increasingly desperate. Our violent society seems to be locked into a deadly game of "Can you top this?" Guns and drugs are readily and easily available. Murders and bombings flicker nightly on our television screens, graphically displaying the results of our lust for power and control. Racism and sexism continue to set oppressive conditions for whole communities of people. We curse and hate one another in the name of God. Greed compromises the integrity of legislators, healers, and religious leaders. We have come to expect that we will rarely encounter truthfulness and trustworthiness in our daily lives. Our culture is marked by a pervasive sense of isolation and individualism, and we are losing our knowledge of how to work together in communities for the common good.

This is the world into which Christians are sent as ambassadors. Our charge is to proclaim God's offer of a redemptive alternative. Salvation, as Paul presents it, engages two dimensions: the individual and the community. Christians are invited to be transformed in their own lives by exchanging a self-destructive human point of view for the reconciling mind of Christ as exemplified in Jesus. Further, those who are re-created by such a transformation are called to advocate, assist, and implement the same transformation of all of human society. This is the mission given to the church: to be reconciled and to become agents of reconciliation.

The famous prayer usually attributed to Francis of Assisi provides a compelling statement of the church's mission:

> Lord make me an instrument of thy peace.
> Where there is hatred, let me sow love;
> Where there is doubt, faith;
> Where there is despair, hope;
> Where there is darkness, light;
> And where there is sadness, joy.

Read 2 Corinthians 5:21

For our sake he made him to be sin who knew no sin, so that in him we might become the righteousness of God.

This great passage captures in one sentence Paul's understanding of what God did in the Christ event. There are at least two essential theological concepts in the passage: **the sinlessness of Jesus** and **the righteousness of God**.

It has often been noted that Paul almost never quoted any of the teachings of Jesus, the Sermon on the Mount, or the parables. Nor did he refer to any event in the life and ministry of Jesus outside of the Lord's Supper, the Crucifixion, and the Resurrection. Paul was insistent, however, upon the full humanity of Jesus. Paul described Jesus as "born of a woman, born under the law" (Galatians 4:4) and "descended from David according to the flesh" (Romans 1:3). In Philippians 2:7, Paul declared that Christ emptied himself of his divinity, "taking the form of a slave, being born in human likeness." Paul's image of Jesus was not a miracle-working divine creature in human flesh, but a truly human person who was perfectly aligned with the will and way of God.

What did Paul mean when he claimed that Jesus "knew no sin" (2 Corinthians 5:21)? Jesus was what every human person is meant to be: a co-creator with God. He saw the world from God's perspective. His values reflected God's values.

What did Paul mean when he claimed that "he made him to be sin" (2 Corinthians 5:21)? Obviously Jesus did not go against God and was not personally alienated from God. But as a human being, Jesus experienced the consequences of sin. Just as all of us do, he inherited and lived in an alienated world characterized by a human point of view; therefore he participated in sin and death.

This is the meaning of the cross. God removed the barrier of guilt created by the exercise of human freedom in opposition to God. Christ on the cross was God's declaration that human freedom is acceptable to God. God in Christ paid a heavy price for that declaration. Even though sinless, he bore the consequences of sin.

The other essential theological concept in the passage is **the righteousness of God**. For Paul, righteousness was not a high degree of conformity to the commandments and moral laws. He saw righteousness as an attitude, a correct orientation, a frame of mind that was aligned with the will and way of God. To be righteous was to see the world as God saw it and to evaluate things with God's values.

When this is understood, it makes sense to talk of us "having the righteousness of God." Being righteous by conforming to the commandments really amounts to self-righteousness. Pauline ethics is not based on behavior but on character. Righteousness consists not so much of good deeds or correct actions as of integrity, good intentions, and pure motives. Thus the only authentic righteousness, the only right orientation to life, is God's righteousness.

In Jesus Christ, God provides the prototype of a righteous human person. Jesus wills what God wills and sees the world as God sees it. In him God's original creation comes to fruition and becomes reality. "Let the same mind be in you that was in Christ Jesus" (Philippians 2:5). When such a transformation of perspective occurs, we become reconciled to our Creator; and we become agents of reconciliation in a broken world.

THE MISSION OF THE CHURCH

• Moving to yet another powerful image for the church, Paul tells the faithful they are ambassadors for Christ. What does this mean? • How would you describe the world into which ambassadors are sent?

• Paul does not think of this ambassadorship as voluntary but as an obligation placed on us by our claim to be Christians. What is our charge? • What does this have to do with being agents of reconciliation? • Do you feel up to the challenge? • Where do you find the courage and support to be an ambassador for Christ? • How do you support others?

• How do you understand Jesus as one made "to be sin" and also one "who knew no sin"? • How did Jesus participate in sin and death? • What does Paul say is the meaning, then, of the cross? •How does this sacrifice make you feel?

• Explore the "righteousness of God." What does Paul say about this? • Besides Jesus, what would a human life look like that had become the righteousness of God? • Have you become the righteousness of God? If not, could you? Explain.

IN CLOSING

• Paul invites us to have the same mind that was in Christ, which marks the fruition of reconciliation with God and the ability to become agents of reconciliation (ambassadors) in a broken world. How have your insights from this session and from this study led you to a closer relationship with God? • What has inspired and motivated you? What has confused you? What questions remain? • What will you do to seek answers and direction? • Who will go with you on your own journey of faith?
• Take time to consider making or renewing your commitment to Jesus Christ. • Pray for the body of Christ and for those who do not know Christ.
• Ask for discernment and direction to be an ambassador for Christ and give thanks for the gifts God has given you.